kitchens

the *smart* approach to design

CRE▲TIVE
HOMEOWNER®

kitchens

the *smart* approach to design

CREATIVE HOMEOWNER®, Upper Saddle River, New Jersey

KITCHENS: THE SMART APPROACH TO DESIGN

SENIOR EDITOR	Kathie Robitz
PROOFREADER	Sara M. Markowitz
PHOTO COORDINATOR, DIGITAL IMAGING	Mary Dolan
INDEXER	Schroeder Indexing Services
INTERIOR DESIGN CONCEPT	Glee Barre, David Geer
COVER DESIGN CONCEPT	Glee Barre
LAYOUT	Kathryn Wityk
FRONT COVER PHOTOGRAPHY	Olson Photographic, LLC
BACK COVER PHOTOGRAPHY	*top* davidduncanlivingston.com; *bottom* courtesy of Wolf

CREATIVE HOMEOWNER

VICE PRESIDENT AND PUBLISHER	Timothy O. Bakke
MANAGING EDITOR	Fran J. Donegan
ART DIRECTOR	David Geer
PRODUCTION COORDINATOR	Sara M. Markowitz

Current Printing (last digit)
10 9 8 7 6 5 4 3 2 1

Manufactured in the United States of America

Kitchens: The Smart Approach to Design
Library of Congress Control Number: 2009925794
ISBN-10: 1-58011-473-3
ISBN-13: 978-1-58011-473-8

CREATIVE HOMEOWNER®
A Division of Federal Marketing Corp.
24 Park Way
Upper Saddle River, NJ 07458
www.creativehomeowner.com

acknowledgments

The editors wish to thank designers Helene Goodman, IIDA;
Susan Obercian, of Europen Country Kitchens; and Lucianna Samu
for their contributions to this book.

We would also like to acknowledge the helpful information
provided by the National Kitchen and Bath Association.

contents

introduction

A kitchen is often referred to as "the heart of the home." It is a room that draws people together—everyone wants to linger there, particularly with friends and family. Therefore, it is important that your kitchen addresses your daily lifestyle and needs. Where should your appliances be located for maximum efficiency? Do you have a preferred countertop material? What is the best layout for within your home? *Kitchens: The Smart Approach to Design* is here to answer these questions, and many more. Here, you'll find a wealth of information on designing your kitchen to fit *you*. Let's get started!

You can make your kitchen warm and welcoming without sacrificing efficiency.

chapter 1

let's get started

Even in today's tighten-your-wallet times, updating your kitchen is an approachable venture. In this chapter, you'll find helpful information on all you'll need to know about planning for your remodel, including which professionals you should contact and whether they should be licensed, obtaining permits, and insurance issues. Whether you will be simply updating your cabinets or planning significant structural changes, your dream kitchen will be even closer to reality after creating a plan.

There's always room for improvement, especially when it comes to an outdated kitchen. Are you ready to take the plunge?

All the Right Moves

The road to an efficient plan will be full of important decisions about who will actually do the work and what it will cost. After all, the space you want to create may very well not only cater to you and your family's cooking and dining habits but also provide a place for you to pay the bills, the children to do their homework, or the entire family to indulge in hobbies. It's fine to window-shop, comb through books and magazines filled with appealing pictures, and make lists of all the things you want your new kitchen to be. While committing to a remodeling project of this size can be intimidating and exciting at the same time, don't allow either your enthusiasm or concerns to cloud your way.

To remain objective and keep from feeling over-whelmed, don't think about everything at once. Take it easy; if you do your research and plan wisely, you'll gain the confidence you need to make smart choices for both your lifestyle and your budget.

Of course, it's important to know all of your options with respect to cabinet styles and finishes, countertop materials, appliances, and all of the other finishing materials and product choices that are on the market, but getting a handle on the more mundane aspects of your project—the amount of work that will be entailed, who will do it, how much time and money it will take, and how to get financing if you need it—is key to your success. In this chapter, you'll find out what you should know about managing your kitchen project, right from the start.

Layout, construction, product and material selection, and installation are all key factors in the success of the kitchen pictured on this page and the one opposite. Good planning and choosing the right professionals should help you achieve your goal while staying within your means.

That's Life!

Remodeling is stressful. It's hard to deal with the sawdust and noise and constant inconvenience of not having a finished kitchen. At times it will seem as though the project is something that is being done to you, rather than for you. But there are ways to ready yourself and your family for the temporary upheaval that could last weeks or even a few months.

Begin by talking to everyone in the family about what is involved. If strangers will be in your home, let your family meet them before the project begins. Your house is your most personal asset and your most private retreat. It is essential that you and your family know how to protect it and yourselves before there are unfamiliar faces walking in and around the place. Also, plan ahead for times when the kitchen is completely off limits. Include a stipend in your budget for restaurant meals and take-out food.

Contractors often talk of what they call the "remodeling curve"—the wave of ups and downs everyone involved in remodeling experiences. Some days are good (such when the framing is done) and some days are bad (when it looks as though nothing has happened in days). This is normal. Prepare for it. Get away when you feel as if nothing is going the way you would like, even if it's just for the weekend.

go green

PROFESSIONALS
Check the Internet for architects and builders who specialize in green projects. Start with www.gbci.org, the Green Building Certification Web site.

Your kitchen renovation may entail adding on or enlarging space, or it can simply be a cosmetic remodel. The kitchen pictured above and on the opposite page demonstrates how much you can improve the function of a modest-size space by opening it up and retrofitting it with high-quality appliances, sleek fixtures, and a handsome countertop.

STEP 1 architects

If you're planning a significant structural change in your kitchen, consulting an architect is a wise move. Be sure to find one who specializes in residential design. (However, if you are a serious cook who often prepares meals for large groups, a commercial architect who specializes in restaurant planning and would be willing to work on a small project might be an option.) Look for the letters "AIA" after an architect's name. This indicates his or her membership in the American Institute of Architects, a national organization of licensed professionals with local and state chapters that readily offer referral services.

STEP 2 CKDs

Certified Kitchen Designers, or CKDs, are trained professionals who are certified specifically in kitchen design and remodeling by the National Kitchen and Bath Association (NKBA). Because they are specialists, they can advise you with regard to spatial issues and layout, as well as offer you advice about the latest trends and innovations in kitchen products that would best suit your needs and lifestyle. Check local cabinet companies, kitchen and bath dealers, or home centers to find a qualified designer—with the letters "CKD" after his or her name. Or log on to www.NKBA.org for a referral.

STEP 3 interior designers

Interior designers do not make structural changes but work with color, pattern, texture, and furnishings to shape a design. He or she will collaborate with an architect or other remodeling professional to create an overall look for your kitchen. You may want to contact an interior designer if you are making significant cosmetic changes to your kitchen. The letters "ASID" after an interior designer's name indicate membership in the American Society of Interior Designers, a national organization of qualified licensed professionals. Your local or state chapter can refer you to an ASID member in your area.

STEP 4 contractors

A contractor is a good choice if you have already hired an architect to design the kitchen or if you are not making substantial structural changes to the room. One good example of when to choose a remodeling contractor is when you are simply refacing cabinets or reconfiguring the existing space for a better layout.

■ **Design-build remodeling firms** are companies that offer one-stop shopping for design services and construction provided by designers and remodelers who are on staff. If something goes wrong, you only have to make one call. There's no buck-passing here.

The owner of the kitchen on this and the opposite page hired an interior designer to help her achieve a specific style. An interior designer can assist you with coordinating cabinetry, finishing materials, colors, and furnishings in order to create a cohesive look.

Budget Matters

This is the not-so-fun part of planning your project—finding and parting with money. No one likes to crunch numbers, but establishing a budget is the only way to determine the scope of your project. It is disappointing to plan a state-of-the-art kitchen that could rival any well-known chef's, only to find that you can barely afford a new cooktop and fresh paint. Don't shy away from big dreams, just determine what you can realistically spend. Get estimates from everyone—and expect to spend more. Build in a buffer—some experts say at least 20 percent—when you're budgeting because most projects end up costing more than planned.

Also, try to avoid paying cash for remodeling. If it comes down to a choice between paying cash for a new kitchen or a car, it makes more sense to finance the remodeling. You can deduct the interest of the remodeling loan from your taxes; you can't deduct the interest on a car.

Financing

Any bank or lending institution will be happy to tell you how much you can afford to spend on your home-remodeling project. But if you feel more comfortable running a test on your own, here is a quick and simple overview of how banks figure out what you can spend.

The debt-to-income (DTI) ratio

This tells a lender if you can handle more debt on your current level of income. While each lender has its own approved DTI ratio, the average is normally at least 45 percent.

Current monthly expenses	$_____
Add the estimated monthly	
remodeling payment	+_____
Total expenses	$_____
Divide by your gross monthly income	÷_____
This is your DTI	_____%

How to find your maximum payment for remodeling

If your DTI doesn't qualify for financing options, you may need to lower the monthly remodeling expenditure. This calculation will show you how low you need to go.

Gross monthly income	$_____
Multiply by lender's DTI ratio	x_____
Subtotal	$_____
Subtract your total monthly expenses	
(minus the estimated remodeling payment)	−_____
This gives you your maximum payment of	$_____

If the last line is negative, you may have to scale back your plans or do the work yourself on a very tight budget. A negative number means that you won't be receiving funds from a lender. However, you can check out other funding options. For example, a consolidation loan will allow you to incorporate your current debts into your home-improvement loan. Firstly, this will lower the monthly cost of your current debts. Secondly, this loan allows you to deduct the interest from your taxes, something that you can't do with other forms of debt.

Today's financial market offers a variety of other forms of financing, as long as your credit score is good. Talk to your lender. You could take out a loan against investments, borrow against your credit card, or obtain a private loan from a family member.

How do I hire someone for my project? Can I get a guarantee? What happens if I change my mind after hiring someone?

what the experts say

The National Association of the Remodeling Industry (NARI), says, "Employ a home-improvement contractor in your area. Local firms can be checked through references from past customers or through your local Better Business Bureau. Local remodelers are compelled to perform quality work that satisfies their customers for their business to survive."

what real people do

When John and Pat decided to renovate their 50-year-old kitchen, they asked a few of their neighbors whether they could recommend a local contractor for the job. After getting estimates and references from several remodeling companies in their area, John and Pat hired someone. A day later they found someone else who was willing to do the job for less. Now what? They had a signed contract with the first contractor. Was it too late to back out of the agreement? Not necessarily.

As one of the contractual parties, they had certain rights, which included changing their minds. This is called the "Right of Rescission," which allows you to change your mind within three days of signing a contract without any liability if the contract was obtained some place other than the contractor's office—their home, for example. This grace period protects you against hasty decisions and hard sells. Federal law mandates making consumers aware of this. Ask your contractor about it.

Legal Issues

You have the right to a specific and binding contract. The more details and pages it has, the better. If it isn't in writing ...

Your contract should include basic items, such as the contractor's business license number; details of what the contractor will and will not do; a detailed list of all materials; an approximate start date and completion dates of various parts of the work; procedures for handling changes, called a "Change Order"; a binding arbitration clause (in case of a disagreement); and a provision for statements and waivers of liens from to be provided to you by the contractor prior to final payment.

Most importantly, be sure you understand all the components of the contract before signing—and never sign an incomplete contract.

Every aspect of this kitchen's striking design, as illustrated opposite, left, and below, had to be agreed upon by the home-owner in writing. Also, any request for modifications of the plans required a written "change order."

Licenses, Insurance, and Permits

Ask to see the remodeler's license if your local or state government requires one. However, just seeing it is not enough. It normally won't show expiration or suspension notices. Call the licensing authority to verify the status of the license.

All contractors should have current liability insurance and worker's compensation. The insurance protects employees of the remodeling firm while they are working on your property, so it pays to check it out before you allow possibly uninsured workers to place themselves in hazardous situations in and around your home. If you are still worried about your liability should an injury occur, talk to your insurance carrier and attorney. You may want to adjust your homeowner's coverage during the project.

Also, never allow the work on your home to be done without the necessary permits. Permits may cost money and require inspections, but they can save you thousands in the future. In some states, if you have any work done without one and a problem occurs, you are held responsible. If faulty electrical work done during your kitchen remodeling is to blame for it, the insurance company can refuse to pay the claim if there is no permit on record. This could be disastrous if the entire house burns down. Remember: nowhere in the home is the possibility of fire more likely than in the kitchen, where more building codes exist than for any other room. By obtaining a permit for your remodeling project, you are guaranteeing that a qualified third party will inspect the work to make sure it complies with all of the required safety regulations.

do this... not that

hands off

If your contractor asks you to apply for the permit yourself, refuse. Most jurisdictions consider the person who obtained the permit to be the one responsible for the outcome of the job. The officials in your jurisdiction will come to you if the work is not up to code during the inspection. If they have a problem, it is far better to let them talk to a professional.

Some jobs, such as electrical and plumbing, require that a licensed professional do the work. If you are doing any of the work yourself, find out the laws in your area.

Tiling a backsplash is one job that a subcontractor may be hired to do. Make sure that your general contractor releases you of any liability, in writing, for any worker who may be injured while on the job. But review your homeowner's insurance, as well.

Take Charge

I t's your house and your money. Don't hesitate to ask as many questions as you like about any detail concerning the project. The more information you have, the happier you will be with the result. This is particularly true when selecting products or figuring out warranty coverage. Find out what is allowed under any warranties and what is forbidden. Many manufacturers won't honor a warranty on an amateur "fix-it" job. To avoid disasters, call your contractor or the manufacturer for guidance.

Make your contractor sign for all deliveries during a job unless you personally ordered the materials or are prepared to be liable for them if the wrong thing is delivered or if something is damaged. Signing for materials is the contractor's responsibility. Imagine what would happen if you signed for an incomplete shipment or the wrong-size floor tiles. That's right, you're responsible for the mistake. Don't take chances. Let your contractor shoulder the burden of tracking down incomplete or damaged orders.

Also, the people you hire to work on your house are in your home. You have every right to tell them not to smoke, play music, curse, or eat inside. You even have the right to tell them where to park and how to store their tools and materials around the place. Establish a set of rules before the work begins, and ask the general contractor to enforce them. Otherwise, do it yourself. Include your rules as part of the contract so you have a vantage point from which to operate.

Finally, decide how you are going to convey problems to your contractor. If you know how you will respond if something goes wrong, you won't panic. If you don't handle stress well, someone else in the household should take over the day-to-day communication with the contractor; maybe your talents could be better spent in the planning stages and the final decor.

for more information
@ **www.NKBA.org**
www.NARI.org

2 budget realistically

10 repurpose

the top **10**
Up-Front Pointers

1 do your homework
Consider what you'd like to achieve with your project.

2 budget realistically Buy the best you can afford and splurge wisely. If you must have a granite countertop, postpone tiling the backsplash, perhaps.

4 hire the right pro

3 be flexible and creative
Depending on the scope of your project, your home will be disrupted for a time that could extend anywhere from two weeks to many months. Where can you set up a temporary kitchen with a refrigerator, a microwave, a coffeemaker, and a hot plate?

4 hire the right professional
Don't hire your brother-in-law's cousin who is a roofer to install your cabinets because "he's so handy, he can do anything." Jobs that particularly require a specialist include stone countertop installation, anything electrical, and some plumbing.

5 put everything in writing
If you don't understand any legalise in your contract, ask a lawyer to explain what it means.

6 look into various sources of financing
Decide what works best for you:
◆ a home equity loan or line of credit
◆ a private loan
◆ your savings

7 expect the unexpected
There's always a glitch or two in the process of remodeling that can affect the timetable or the cost of a project.

You can't anticipate everything, but you should build a cushion into your budget.

8 avoid making changes
After you sign off on a plan, changes become very expensive to make.

9 always get permits
If you don't, you risk a hefty fine and possibly undoing completed work.

10 recycle
Reuse or repurpose. Save the earth and your bank account.

25

DIY?

This analysis is a great idea if you are contemplating doing the renovation yourself. We have all seen the various do-it-yourself (DIY) cable shows that make everything look so easy. But don't forget that those shows are run by professionals who have the tools, experience, skills, and assistants that are necessary to do it successfully the first time. Can you remodel the kitchen on your own? That depends. Take the National Association of the Remodeling Industry (NARI) quiz, opposite, to get an idea of whether or not you should tackle it.

NARI says that if you marked a majority of the answers "yes," you may want to attempt doing the job yourself. But before you strap on a carpenter's belt, revisit those marked "no." Consider the problems you may face in those areas. Hiring a professional may still be your best option. Or you can compromise: hire a professional for the technical and difficult aspects of the job, such as the plumbing or the installation of the cabinets, and do the cosmetic work yourself.

Utilizing your own skills and knowledge can be a great asset to your remodel. Repainting cabinets, such as these, is a fairly simple do-it-yourself job.

Should You Do It Yourself?

Before you make the decision to take on kitchen remodeling project on your own, spend a few minutes answering the following questions. This exercise will help you determine whether or not you have the necessary skills and abilities. Be honest with yourself.

Yes	No	Do you enjoy physical work?
Yes	No	Are you persistent and patient? (Do you have reliable work habits? Once the project is started, will it get finished?)
Yes	No	Do you have all the tools needed and, more importantly, the skills required to do the job?
Yes	No	Are your skills at the level of quality you need for this project?
Yes	No	Do you have time to complete the project? (Always double or triple the time estimated for a DIY project, unless you are highly skilled and familiar with that type of project.)
Yes	No	Will it matter if the project remains unfinished for a period of time?
Yes	No	Are you prepared to handle the kind of stress this project will create in your family relationships?
Yes	No	Have you done all of the steps involved in the project before?
Yes	No	Have you obtained the installation instructions from the manufacturers of the various products and fixtures to determine whether this is a project you still want to undertake? (You can obtain them from most manufacturers before purchase to determine the steps involved in installation and the skill level required.)
Yes	No	Is this a job that you can accomplish completely by yourself, or will you need assistance? (If you'll need help, what skill level is involved for your assistant? If you need a professional subcontractor, do you have access to a skilled labor pool?)
Yes	No	Are you familiar with local building codes and permit requirements? (Check into these matters before beginning work on your kitchen project.)
Yes	No	What will you do if something goes wrong and you can't handle it? (Most contractors are wary about taking on a botched DIY job, and many just won't. The liability is too high.)
Yes	No	Is it safe for you to do this project? (If you are unfamiliar with roofing [for a kitchen addition] or do not have fall-protection restraints, you may not want to venture a roofing job. Similarly, if you know nothing about electricity, leave it to the professionals. Some jobs can have serious consequences if not performed correctly. Your health and safety should be the primary concerns.)
Yes	No	Can you obtain the materials you need? (Who will be your supplier?)
Yes	No	Are you attempting to do it yourself for financial reasons? (If so, have you looked at all your costs, including the cost of materials, your time, and the tools you need to purchase? If you are new to the DIY game, you may also want to consider the cost to correct any mistakes you may make. Will it still be a cost-saving venture given all of these factors?)
Yes	No	If you are trying DIY for your personal satisfaction, can you really guarantee a job that will be well done? (If it doesn't come out right, how will you feel? Will you need the money to redo any unsatisfactory work? Will you have it? Will you be able to live with mistakes?)

There are so many factors that contribute to an attractive, cohesive design, but planning is number one. In this multizone kitchen, both the homeowner and designer considered how the family would work and live in the space before any products were purchased or even before the physical layout was put on paper. **Far right:** The homeowner wanted a large island for food prep as well as for informal meals. **Top right:** Because the family entertains, professional-style

it's in the details *

appliances make sense. **Right:** A separate sink and dishwasher drawer near serving pieces and stemware storage organizes cleanup tasks.

let's get started

kitchen layouts

The size of your kitchen and the amount of money you can spend on it doesn't necessarily guarantee a great design. Function is key, and you can expect your new kitchen to be efficient when the layout makes sense, even if it's small. One wall, galley, U-, L-, or G-shaped, which one is right for you? Will you include an island or peninsula in your plans? Will it be the classic eat-in kitchen? Here's what you need to know.

A kitchen layout should cater to your cooking routine and how you want to live in the space.

Kitchen Design, Your Way

Function is the cornerstone of good kitchen design. A highly functional kitchen will not necessarily make you a master chef, but it will improve the quality of the time you spend there, which some experts report can be as much as 70 percent of your waking hours. So decide early what you would like your kitchen to be—gourmet central, family headquarters, baker's paradise, the place to party, or simply a heat-it-and-eat-it joint. Your lifestyle, food preferences, and cooking style are all to be considered.

Design professionals interview their clients at length at the beginning of a project. If you will be your own designer, do the same. Some questions to ask yourself include: How often do you cook as opposed to dining out? Do you typically cook meals from scratch? Do you like to interact with people while preparing a meal? Is there adequate cabinet storage in your current kitchen? How often do you grocery shop? How does the existing floor plan work for you? Do you often cook with another person? Are there too many steps between the sink, cooktop, and refrigerator? Is there enough room for opening the refrigerator door when someone passes behind you? Anything else that obstructs the aisles in the work area?

Don't forget to consider how you—and other family members—prefer to take your meals; today, many families forgo the formal dining room for an eat-in kitchen with a place for quick snacks at the kitchen island.

Make a list of upgrades or amenities that could make your kitchen more functional—a second dishwasher, desk, or wine storage, for example.

Design for specific tasks. A refrigerator drawer, above, under the counter where you'll be rinsing and chopping vegetables is a smart idea. A convenient pot filler faucet above the cooktop, below, saves steps. Locate ovens near the cooktop, opposite, if you can.

What if...

Space has its limitations, of course, and you may have to build an addition, which will raise your budget significantly. If that's out of the question, look at adjacent spaces, such as hallways, pantries, under the stairs, or even an adjoining room. You may be able to open up the layout or create enough floor space to accommodate an island or peninsula by removing a nonload-bearing wall.

You can also recess appliances and set custom cabinets as much as 4 to 6 inches into the wall between wall studs. This doesn't sound like much of a space gain, but 6 inches on each side of a room may yield enough additional square footage for an efficient work triangle.

Don't limit your search for extra space to the interior living areas of your house. Take over the garage or the back porch. You'll have to weatherize them, but that project is considerably less expensive than building an addition.

If you're planning to extend a stone or solid-surface countertop for a snack bar, you'll need to support it with brackets if the overhang is over 12 in.

Squeeze Play

Short on space? You can still make your kitchen efficient and easy to keep organized. Remember, no kitchen layout is absolutely perfect!

■ A small island or peninsula can beef up function. Consider a small table on wheels that lock in place. You can move it out of the way when not in use or let it double as a dining table.

■ Hang pots and pans from a rack. Even a somewhat disorganized arrangement of these accoutrements can add charm to your kitchen.

■ Install open shelves for display and storage.

Keeping cabinets and most surfaces white makes this small kitchen airy and bright. There's a spacious pantry behind these doors, right. An extra-deep sink and high-arc faucet, below, make it easy to wash large pots and platters.

Clearly defined zones make good use of space in this kitchen. **Far right:** Designed with the classic work triangle in mind, the compact work area places the cooktop at the center point with the refrigerator and sink (not pictured) at points opposite from one another. The back of the banquette serves as a half wall between the food preparation and dining areas. **Top right:** The decorative use of small glass tiles behind the glass cooktop makes this

it's in the details ✳

zone the center of attention. **Right:** For added storage, there is a horizontal row of cabinets with flip-up doors over the banquette that look chic and contemporary.

find flip-up doors

@ www.kraftmaid.com
www.almillmo-us.com

I am thinking of enlarging my 13- x 10-foot kitchen by extending it into my dining room. What should I consider?

what the experts say

"First, find out whether you have to remove a load-bearing wall or not. If so, leave that job to a framing professional," say the experts at the National Kitchen and Bath Association. **"Another concern would be the type of floor in the new kitchen. A concrete slab would make electrical, ducting, and plumbing changes difficult."**

Decide how you want to use the space. **"Larger kitchens allow for additional kitchen centers."**

what real people do

There is a common mistake people make in this situation when they don't have professional design advice—they spread out the major appliances. Good kitchen design *reduces* the cook's steps between the cooktop or range and the sink and refrigerator. A better solution would be to create several centers or zones, a separate one for baking or entertaining, for example. Include a second sink, perhaps another dishwasher, or an undercounter refrigerator or wine cooler.

An island can be a great addition to a kitchen, as long as it is the right size for the space and is located so that it doesn't obstruct anything.

Creating a Layout

All you may be thinking of doing is updating appliances, replacing cabinetry, and installing new flooring, countertops, and wallpaper. But you may want to think about modifying the layout, at least on paper. You may be surprised to see how much a few minor changes in your floor plan can improve your original layout. Would the space function better if you moved a doorway or removed a nonload-bearing wall? (If the wall is load bearing, you will have to add a beam for structural support. Discuss this with a professional before getting out a sledgehammer.)

Try sketching different arrangements on paper to see how they would work. Would the layout improve if you could move the gas line for the range or scoot plumbing lines over a foot or two? While structural and service changes add to the cost of the remodel, they could be money well spent if they result in a kitchen that is more functional on a day-to-day basis for years to come.

For ideas, look at the typical kitchen layout configurations on pages 44–59.

In this open plan, the island sink, opposite top, anchors the layout and faces the dining zone and a bank of windows (not pictured). This gives the homeowner a view into the garden while washing dishes. Across the aisle, right, you can see that there are just a few steps between the range and the refrigerator.

smart steps   Plan Like a Pro

STEP 1 measure everything

Measure the length and width of the room and the height of the walls. Then from one corner, measure the location of windows and doors. Record the swing of each door. Write each dimension in inches to the nearest ¼ inch.

■ **Measure cabinetry and appliances.** Also indicate their height. Measure the position and centerline of the sink, showing how far the center is from the wall. You'll also need the sink's overall width and length.

■ **Be thorough.** Include measurements for everything, from the width of every doorway and window to how far the refrigerator protrudes into the room. If there's an island or pensinsula, measure its length, height, and depth. Don't forget to include the kitchen table, too.

■ **Check yourself.** Before proceeding, check and double-check your measurements for accuracy.

STEP 2 draw a floor plan

Do a rough sketch of your layout, and then transfer it to graph paper with grids marked at ¼-inch intervals. This is your "base plan," as it is called, and it should record the layout of the space as it currently exists.

■ **Indicate light fixtures, electrical outlets, and heat registers.** (See the sketch, below left.)

■ **Indicate load-bearing walls.** These walls cannot be moved or removed without compromising structural integrity. If you don't know whether a wall is load-bearing, consult your architect or a qualified contractor. Never guess.

■ **Make notations.** On or next to your sketch, make a list of what you don't like or want to change. Keep in mind that your plan does not have to be professionally drawn, only accurate in its rendition of the current space.

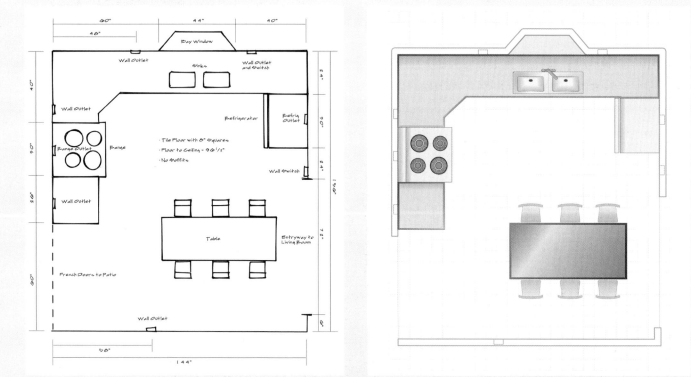

Begin planning by carefully measuring your existing kitchen. Record all dimensions in inches to avoid confusion (left). Transfer the drawing to graph paper (right), and use cutouts to create new layouts.

Zoned for Efficiency

You have probably heard of the work triangle, which places the sink, refrigerator, and cooktop or range at the three points of a triangle to conserve walking distance in a kitchen. Experts recommend that the sum of all three lines of the triangle should be no greater than 26 feet and no less than 12 feet. For a large kitchen, especially where two people cook together, plan two or more work triangles. Although two appliances may share one side of the triangle for maximum performance, do not overlap the sink and range areas. Another option is to design small work zones set within one large triangle.

If your kitchen is large and serves various functions—cooking, dining, home office, hobbies, family room, for example—the room's spatial design will have to embrace these activities. This is when you'll need to consider designing several autonomous triangles within the room.

A center island, above, splits the work area down the middle, separating the food preparation and cleanup zones. Another view of the layout, left, reveals a raised counter for informal meals and snacks.

This spacious eat-in kitchen has a lot going for it. **Far right:** Its U-shaped configuration provides ample built-in storage and counter space. Lively color accents and the pale-wood cabinets keep it light and bright. **Top right:** Across from the table, an island is dedicated solely to cooking. Here's where the work zone begins. To the right, there is a large sink (not pictured); turn around, and there's the refrigerator and ovens. All in all, a convenient arrangement of space.

it's in the
details *

Right: The table's placement lets the kids color or do homework without getting underfoot in the work area. Meanwhile, the dogs patiently anticipate chow time.

One-Wall Kitchen

This arrangement, typical in some apartments, places all the equipment, sink, and cabinetry along one wall. If you want to retain this arrangement but would like to close off the kitchen from other public areas of the home, install sliding doors or screens that can be opened or closed as you wish.

■ **Work zones:** Because you cannot create a triangle in a one-wall kitchen, maximize accessibility by locating the sink between the refrigerator and the range.

Two people can work together here efficiently if you place the sink between the refrigerator and the cooktop or range.

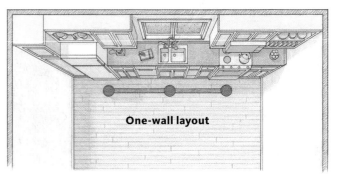

One-wall layout

This one-wall kitchen is located in a converted industrial loft. The dining table can double as a work surface when needed. A six-burner stove, opposite, is at one end, and the refrigerator (not shown) is at the other end of the work area.

Galley Kitchen

This compact layout locates the appliances, sink, and cabinets on two parallel walls to create a small pass-through kitchen. It's easy to configure an efficient work triangle in this setup, but the layout really caters to one cook.

■ **Traffic:** If possible, allow a 48-inch-wide aisle after all the fixtures are in place so that the cabinet and appliance doors can be opened easily while someone walks through the space. You could make the aisle 36 inches wide, but appliance doors may collide with each other if opposite doors are open at the same time.

■ **Storage:** This can be a challenge in a layout that is as compact as a galley. The solution is to install tall cabinets that extend to the ceiling. Reserve the top shelves for seldom-used items.

To avoid traffic problems, locate the refrigerator near the end of the galley.

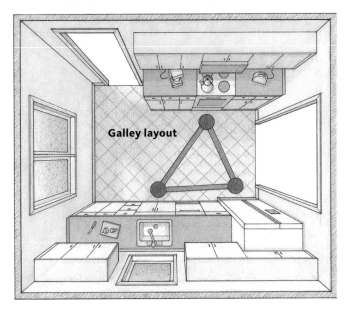

Galley layout

In a galley kitchen, aisle width is particularly important for function and ease.

Traffic flow is facilitated here by locating the sink and the range across from each other.

U-Shape

Some experts believe the U-shaped kitchen is the most efficient design. Cabinets, counters, and appliances are all arranged along three walls in a U configuration. The greatest benefit to this plan is the easy traffic flow.

A U-shaped layout incorporates a logical sequence of work centers with minimum distances between each. The sink is often, but not always, located at the base of the U, with the refrigerator and range on the side walls opposite each other.

■ **Corners:** Corners can create unusable space. However, you can overcome that by angling cabinets into them. Corner units on bottom cabinets with carousel shelves or lazy Susans actually make storage more handy than standard units.

This spacious U-shaped layout is anchored by a large center island. Note that dining is located at the far end of the island away from the work zones.

U-Shaped Configuration

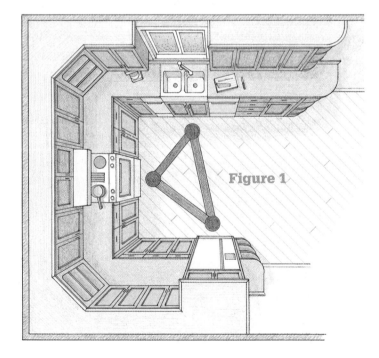

Figure 1

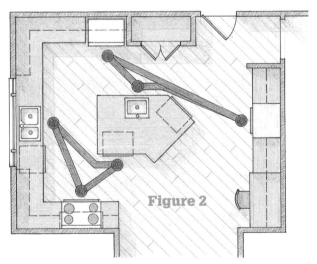

Figure 2

Figure One: A typical U-shaped layout

Figure Two: A large U-shaped kitchen can be expanded to accommodate multiple work triangles.

A second sink for rinsing vegetables or filling pots is located at the end of the island across from the range.

This U-shaped kitchen makes use of both an island and a peninsula. **Far right:** The large, centrally located island is primarily dedicated to dining and serving buffet-style when the family entertains—its spacious surface is perfect for handling large platters of food. Of course, it's also convenient during food preparation, especially as it is near the range and sink. Below-counter refrigerator drawers on the side facing the sink hold fresh produce and chilled drinks.

it's in the
details *

Top right: There is ample landing space on either side of the cooktop for food just coming off the heat. **Right:** Across the room, the peninsula is actually the dinner table.

L-Shape

This plan places the kitchen on two perpendicular walls. The L-shape usually consists of one long and one short "leg" and lends itself to an efficient work triangle without the problem of through traffic. If it's well designed, it's flexible enough for two cooks to work simultaneously without getting in each other's way.

■ **Counters:** Another advantage to an L-shaped layout is the opportunity for incorporating an island into the floor plan if space allows. (Attach a peninsula to one leg of the design, and you've created an F-shaped space.) If you do include an island or peninsula in an L-shaped kitchen, plan the clearances carefully.

L-Shaped Configuration

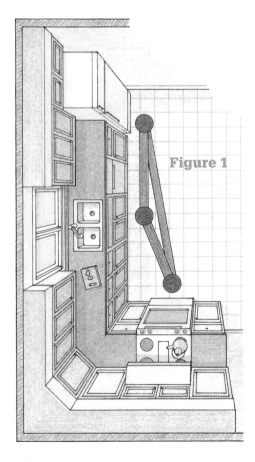

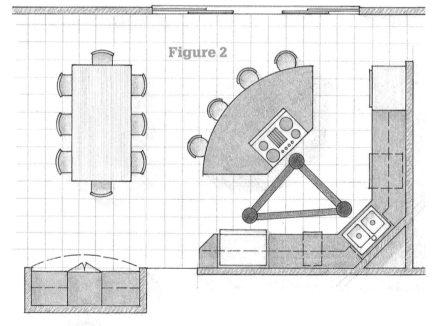

Figure One: A typical L-shaped arrangement.

Figure Two: Installing a curved island diagonally across from an L configuration expands the possibilities of the work triangle.

Here's an example of an L-shaped layout that has incorporated an island. Both the work aisle, above, and the area behind the island seating have been designed with ample clearances for traffic.

This L-shaped work area gets a boost from its island, which anchors what could have been a rambling layout and provides a place for the cooktop, completing a perfect work triangle. **Far right:** With a comfortable overhang, the island counter offers seating out of the work area.

Top right: The designer placed the refrigerator and microwave at the far end of the layout so that family members can grab a drink or heat a snack without bothering the busy cook.

it's in the
details ✳

Right: In what was the breakfast room, a wall was removed to bring lots more natural light into the kitchen. Bertoia-inspired bar stools keep the look airy.

G-Shape

This is a hybrid of the U-shape with a shorter, fourth leg added in the form of a peninsula. While the G-shaped layout is suitable for more than one person working in the kitchen, it may feel confining—particularly with an island located in the center.

This layout may feature a pair of sinks and a separate cooktop, as well as oven ranges. One work triangle usually incorporates a sink, the cooktop, and the refrigerator, while the other houses the second sink, the oven, and, overlapping the first triangle, the refrigerator.

■ **Counters:** The G-shaped kitchen easily accommodates specialty appliances, such as warming drawers, dishwashing drawers, modular refrigeration, or a built-in grill, to allow independence between two or more work areas.

The G-Shaped Configuration

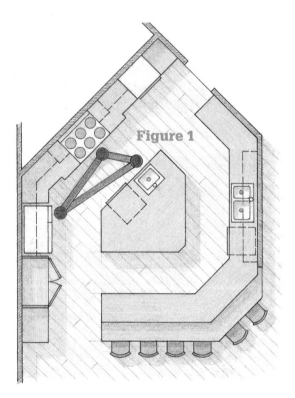

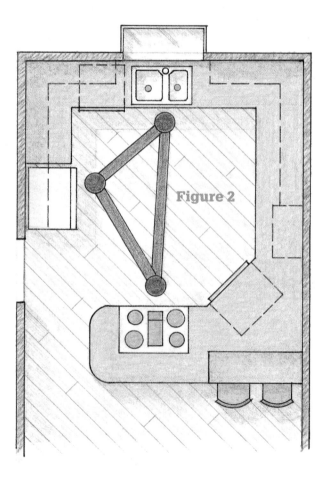

Figure One: A large G-shaped layout allows separate cooking and cleanup areas, with a generous amount of work surfaces.

Figure Two: The typical G configuration is a U with the addition of a short leg—usually a peninsula.

Even in a compact space, you can make the most of a G-shaped layout. In a kitchen that is open to family living space, a glass-fronted cabinet, right, houses attractive serving pieces and pottery. The raised countertop, below, conceals some of the clutter of food preparation and cleanup.

Here's an example of a typical G-shaped layout, a U with the addition of a leg, often a short peninsula. Because the work area is not that large, the designer decided to forgo cabinets on the longest wall (the sink's), and install windows to open up the space.

Far right: Where used, wall cabinets take advantage of the kitchen's sloped ceiling and extend up as far as possible. Dishes and serveware are kept in cabinets surrounding the

it's in the details ✳

range and near the eating bar. **Top right:** Glassware is stored on the opposite wall, near the refrigerator. **Right:** Ample space was left for a roomy cleanup area, which extends the full length of the room.

get more layout help
www.NKBA.org
sketchup.google.com

Islands and Peninsulas

Shorten the distance between the three key work areas by adding an island or peninsula. A peninsula base and ceiling-hung cabinets offer storage for tableware and linens. In an L- or U-shaped kitchen, an island can add visual interest, breaking up the space without confining it. It also provides an extra work surface or dining spot.

An island or peninsula can also serve as an excellent location for a cooktop or second sink if plumbing and ventilation hookups permit.

An island can handle many functions. Besides serving breakfast here most mornings, the homeowner, who bakes as a hobby, uses this marble countertop, left, to roll out dough.

✳ do this... not that

counter seating

If you can't comfortably fit a table and chairs into your kitchen, let the island or peninsula serve double duty as an eating bar. However, a 63-inch-long counter (a typical size) will accommodate three stools at most.

A 28- to 32-inch-high counter requires 18-inch-high chairs with 20 inches of knee space under the bar. If you make the island or peninsula the standard countertop height (36 inches), you'll be able to accommodate 24-inch-high stools and 14 inches of knee space. Go up to bar height (42 to 45 inches), and you'll need 30-inch-high stools with footrests, also with 14 inches of knee space.

At the end of this island, above, the long, deep "trough" sink easily accommodates trays and cookie sheets.

Some Island and Peninsula Configurations

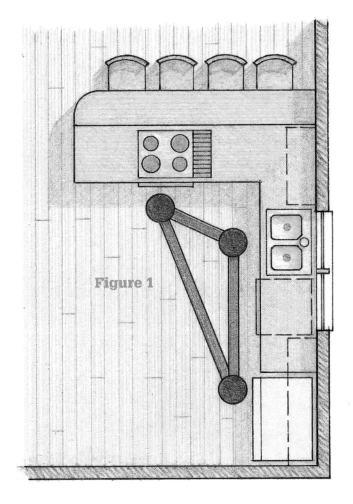

Figure 1

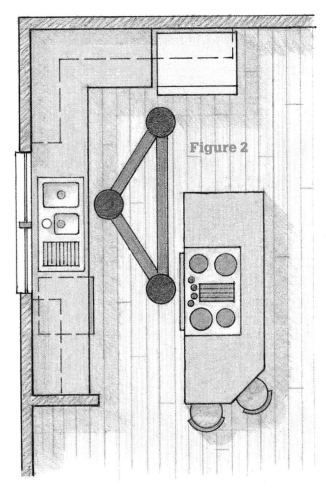

Figure 2

Figure 3

Figure One: Adding a peninsula creates a more-efficient L and provides added storage and dining space.

Figure Two: If space permits, a cooktop can be located in an island, as shown.

Figure Three: Adding a sink and possibly a second dishwasher in an island boosts the efficiency of a secondary work zone.

Is there any way to make a modest kitchen feel less confined without building an extension on to the house?

what the experts say

Look up, recommends award-winning designer Lucianna Samu. In her own spatially challenged kitchen, she blew out the ceiling to the rafters to increase the room's volume. Then she tore down the walls of several small adjacent rooms, incorporating what had been the breakfast room, the laundry, a pantry, and a powder room into the existing kitchen. This gave Lucianna the large new kitchen she desired—with a hearthside sitting area as a bonus—without the expense of an addition.

what real people do

Another way to use vertical space is to build cabinets that extend all the way to the ceiling. This will increase your storage space, especially for seldom-used but important items. However, one thing to remember when doing this is that the sheer mass of it can overwhelm your space. Glass doors on all or some of the upper units or open shelves can alleviate that problem. Serviceability should be important, but should beauty.

Eat-In Kitchens

A family of four will require at least 48 square feet in an eat-in kitchen. Assume that a 36-inch-diameter round table can seat four adults; a 48-inch-diameter one will accommodate six. Calculate 21 to 24 inches of table space per person for a square or rectangular table. Also, pay attention to the distance between the table and the walls or cabinets. A seated adult occupies a depth of about 20 inches from the edge of the table but will need 12 to 16 additional inches of space to push back the chair and rise.

A round table is a smart choice, above, especially when there's a lot of moving about the room. This table takes up a small amount of space, and it has no hard corners. On the other hand, a breakfast bar at the island, opposite, is handy.

cabinets & storage

Cabinets will consume the lion's share of your budget. They'll also define the style and feel of your kitchen—contemporary, modern, traditional, vintage, or a blend. For top of the line, be prepared to spend tens of thousands of dollars. But you can find quality at a more moderate price, depending on the extras—a special finish, custom cabinet interiors, and upgraded hardware are all factors that add to the bottom line. Here's a rundown on the latest trends and styles.

You'll be spending plenty on new cabinets, so it's important to think about how much and the kinds of kitchen storage you need.

Cabinet Types

Traditional-style cabinets have a full frame across the face of the cabinet box that may show between closed doors. This secures adjacent cabinets and strengthens wider cabinet boxes with a center rail. Hinges on framed cabinets may or may not be visible. The doors may be ornamented with raised or recessed panels, trimmed or framed panels, or framed-glass panels.

Frameless cabinets, which are built without a face frame, have a sleek modern look. There's no trim or molding with this simple design. Close-fitting doors cover the entire front of the box; no ornamentation appears on the face of the doors; and hinges are typically hidden inside the cabinet box.

Custom-made cabinets are not limited by size or style; they are built to your specifications and sometimes constructed on-site. Semicustom cabinets are also built to size but by a cabinet company. More-affordable stock cabinets are mass-produced and come in a variety of standard styles, sizes, and options. The most economical, knock-down cabinets require do-it-yourself assembly.

In this modern kitchen, below, extra-deep drawers can hold everything from pots and pans to dishes. Wall units feature flip-up doors. For an updated traditional look, the owners of this kitchen, opposite, selected a square-panel door style.

get smart
PAY FOR QUALITY
The quality of stock cabinets varies by manufacturer, ranging from below adequate to excellent. Inquire about what materials were used, the grade (quality) of the materials, and the type of joinery. Don't buy anything that is simply glued together.

Recessed wall cabinets with flip-up doors keep this kitchen, right, looking sleek.

How can I judge whether the cabinets I choose will hold up over time? Isn't solid wood the best? What if I can't afford it?

what the experts say

Solid wood is too expensive for most of today's budgets, but it can be used on just the doors and frames. More typical is plywood box construction, which offers good structural support, and solid-wood doors and frames. There are other things to look for in quality cabinet construction, including dovetail or mortise-and-tenon joinery and solidly mortised hinges. Also, make sure the interior of every cabinet is well finished, with adjustable shelves that are a minimum ⅜-inch thick to prevent bowing.

what real people do

To save money, cabinetmakers sometimes use strong plywood for support elements, such as the box and frame, and medium-density fiberboard for other parts, such as doors and drawer fronts. In yet another alternative, good-quality laminate cabinets can be made with high-quality, thick particleboard underneath the laminate finish. The material will hold screws securely, and the cabinet won't warp over time.

Because the cooktop takes up most of the work surface in this part of the kitchen, an appliance garage, above, offers a spot for storing cooking utensils that need to be at hand.

Custom cabinets can accommodate any floor plan. One bank of cabinetry lines an entire wall in this large space, left. A stepladder comes in handy for reaching items on high shelves. This one, below, was designed to fit into the toekick area when it's folded.

do this... not that

custom versus semicustom

Custom cabinets can take up to three months to be completed. The wait is worth it: these cabinets look like fine furniture in both their detailing and color. But such craftsmanship isn't cheap. Custom cabinets can be moderately priced or extremely expensive.

Semicustom cabinets take about eight weeks to be delivered and usually, but not always, cost less than custom cabinets, depending on quality, finish, and any extra features you order. Although styles and shapes are standard, semicustom cabinets may come in special sizes and with custom interior organizers and special finishes.

Opposite the work area, racks for storing wine and a custom window seat match the rest of the kitchen cabinetry.

There are serious professional appliances in this kitchen, but they can't detract from the room's overall warmth, thanks to the handsome cherry cabinetry. **Opposite:** The cabinets' lustrous high-gloss finish strikes a pleasing balance with the appliances' cool matte look. **Top right:** Brushed stainless-steel cabinet hardware provides the visual link that unites the wood with everything in the room that is metal.

Bottom right: A stone countertop

it's in the details *

and floor tiles coordinate well with the two materials. They are cool to the touch but have warm flecks of color that pick up similar tones in the wood.

find stainless-steel pulls

@ www.wwhardware.com
www.IKEA.com

Accessorizing Options

Most people would agree that no matter how much storage space they have, they need even more. The problem often isn't the amount, it's the inaccessible placement and inefficient configuration of the storage space. One of the greatest benefits today's designers and manufacturers offer is fitted and accessorized interiors that maximize even the smallest nook and cranny inside cabinets and drawers. These accommodations not only expand the use of space but increase convenience and accessibility. Among them are appliance garages; built-in pantry units; lazy Susans and carousel shelves; fold-down, slide-, and tilt-out trays, racks, and shelves; lid and sheet-pan organizers; extra-deep and wide drawers; and compartmentalized drawer interiors.

2 leftover space

the top 10 Organizers

1 pantries Don't have the space for a walk-in pantry? A built-in pantry cabinet can put narrow spaces to good use. Other built-in types may consist of shelves on the inside of the cabinet doors, plus pullout or foldout shelves inside the cabinet.

2 leftover space Use shallow spaces and toekick areas.

4 open bins

7 extra-large drawers

5 vertical storage

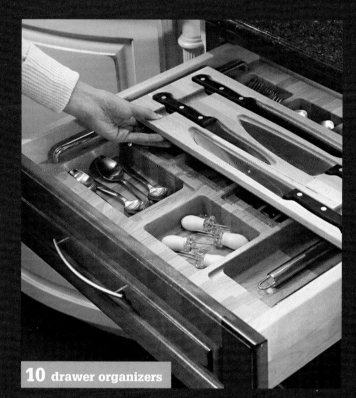

10 drawer organizers

3 pullouts and revolving units
Bins, shelves, and trays that roll out make even items at the back of a cabinet easy to find. Glide-out shelves make excellent storage for small appliances, too. Lazy Susans and carousel shelves utilize corner space.

4 open bins Wire bins or baskets that glide out are perfect for storing
- potatoes
- onions
- garlic bulbs
- some fruits, such as apples.

5 vertical storage Trays, cookie sheets, and platters are so much more accessible when stored vertically rather than stacked.

6 flip-up doors Upper-cabinet doors come with hinges that allow the door to stay open and out of your way.

7 extra-large drawers These extra-long and -deep drawers glide out easily, can be compartmentalized, and can hold a set of dishes or large pots, pans, lids, and small appliances.

8 pull-down shelves Perfect for hard-to-reach spots, pull-down shelves bring an upper cabinet's contents down to your height, and then fold back up and into the cabinet box.

9 sink cabinets
- a drop-down compartment in the shallow area in front of the sink for sponges
- U-shaped pullout that fits under or around the pipes
- a pulllout caddy

10 drawer organizers
- two-tier organizers
- knife racks
- spice racks
- organizers for plastic wrap, wine bottles, et cetera.

A glide-out pantry unit, left, offers easy-to-access storage for everything from pasta to bread crumbs. A shallow but wide drawer near the ovens, below, keeps towels and oven mitts handy when needed.

do this... not that

use what you have

Smart design makes good use of every square inch of space. How can you make use of a corner? (Install a lazy Susan or carousel shelves; angle an appliance garage in it.) Don't leave wasted space above cabinets—take them to the top of the wall. Use the toekick area for shallow drawers that you can use for trays or cookie sheets. Look around; you may have more usable space than you think.

Even narrow space is usable. This homeowner uses it to store wine. Construction is easy; ask your contractor about doing something similar.

Because the cabinetry selected by the homeowner is dark, the designer of this kitchen refrained from installing a lot of wall units, reserving them for one small area. **Far right:** Whatever was sacrificed in the bargain was regained within the large L-shaped peninsula.

Top right: Large appliances, such as the wall ovens, can be tucked inside nooks or built in to leave more room for traffic.

Bottom right: Smart use of small space within cabinet

it's in the details *

interiors includes glide-out units and a place for a roll of paper towels off the countertop but handy near the sink.

cabinets & storage

STEP 1 analyze your needs

Make a detailed list of your shopping and cooking habits. If you buy in bulk, how much of it has to be stored in the refrigerator? Do you need special storage for wines or bottled vinegars? Canned goods, boxed grains, and pasta will need cabinet space.

■ **Cooking and serving items.** Where are you most likely to use them? In the preparation area? By the cooktop? In both places?

■ **Small appliances.** Are they handheld or larger? Heavy or awkward to move? How often do you use them? Do you want them off the countertop?

STEP 2 compartmentalize

Make a plan now to store similar items, such as all baking pans on one shelf, all cookbooks in one spot. Plan to store cooking utensils in one or two drawers near prep areas and to keep all of the pots and pans together.

■ **Shelve foods by type.** For example, keep all the cereals in one area, all the snack foods in another, and all beverages together.

Plan now to tailor your shelf heights to meet these needs by measuring boxes and cans. Not only will this maximize the use of cabinet space, it will make finding what you need quicker and easier.

STEP 3 accessorize

Some of the interior cabinet options discussed earlier can drive up costs, but there are other, less-expensive accessories that can keep items neatly organized when cabinet space is at a premium.

Besides the ubiquitous wire shelf and bin options, a wall- or ceiling-mounted pot rack can make use of otherwise overlooked overhead space. A knife rack that attaches to the wall or the outside of a cabinet is also handy. Wall racks that hold wine, barware, spices, mops and brooms, and ironing boards are negligible in price but invaluable space savers.

STEP 4 make recycling easy

Don't make recycling an afterthought. If you don't want to run outdoors to the various recycling receptacles, try to incorporate a place in the kitchen to unobtrusively separate and contain recyclable items, such as bottles, cans, and paper.

■ **Slide-out bins.** Plastic receptacles in slide-out drawers are an excellent solution if you can spare the cabinet space. In some kitchens a slide-out can accommodate two containers: the one in front is reserved for nonrecyclables, such as food scraps; the second container is solely for recyclable trash.

Establishing Style with Cabinets

Think of your cabinets as furniture for your kitchen. The style you select will set the tone for the overall look of the room.

Start by selecting a door style. Kitchen showrooms and home-improvement centers will be able to show you many examples.

If your taste leans toward traditional, look at the various types of paneled doors—reveal overlay, raised, cathedral, curved, frame and panel, beaded frame and panel, and so forth. A reveal-overlay panel or a beaded frame and panel are decorative and fit in well with an Old World look, whereas the simpler frame-and-panel door style suits a Shaker- or cottage-inspired design. On the other hand, a flat-panel door style is a hallmark of contemporary or modern design.

Finish is another way to pull together a look and coordinate the kitchen with the rest of the house. Dark finishes have an edge over light natural and white finishes today, but the latter are still popular, whichever your style.

Handsome Hardware

Sleek metallic bars add the finishing touch to contemporary or modern cabinets, and they are available in all price points. Classic pulls and knobs in reproduction styles dress up traditional cabinets.

Whatever the style, cabinet hardware comes in numerous finishes—nickel, stainless steel, pewter, chrome, and bronze, to name a few—and may be polished, matte, or hammered. Besides metal, wood, glass, plastic, and even rubber are other possibilities.

References in the cabinetry to both Craftsman and Asian architecture and design are distinctive in this Pacific Northwest kitchen, opposite.

White paneled cabinets, above, give this kitchen an updated look that still retains its cottage-style charm. For something more contemporary, the owners of this kitchen, below, selected a flat-panel door style but chose a medium wood tone for its appealing warmth.

Popular with many people today, transitional-style cabinets combine elements of both traditional and contemporary design. It's a sophisticated way to get the best of both points of view.

Right: These custom cabinets have a clean-lined look with a few references to classical architecture.

Opposite top: Crown molding and columns, though traditional, are done simply and without extra ornamentation.

Opposite middle: The same is true of

it's in the details ✳

the cabinet hardware, which has a rustic handforged look.

Opposite bottom: the room's open floor plan and furnishings reinforce the essentially of-the-moment look.

cabinets & storage

chapter 4

surfaces

- THE TOP 10 SURFACE TRENDS
- COUNTERTOPS AND BACKSPLASHES
- IT'S IN THE DETAILS
- SMART FLOORING CHOICES
- CEILING TREATMENTS

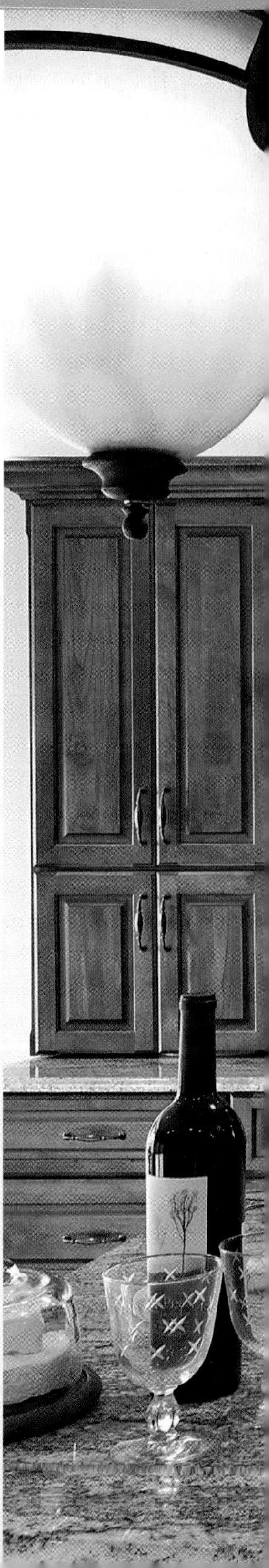

Now that you've chosen your floor plan and cabinetry, you can move on to other important details, such as selecting the materials for the surfaces in your new kitchen. In particular, the countertops and floors play a large role that is not only about function but also about feeling. Think about rolling dough over a cool-to-the-touch marble surface or standing barefoot on a wood floor. Need more ideas? Here are your options.

Make informed choices when you select the materials for the surfaces in your kitchen.

6 quartz

8 solid surfacing

the top 10
Surface Trends

1 **mixing materials** Combining cool metal and stone with warm wood adds depth to a design.

2 **glass** Look for this luminous material on cooktops, appliance fronts, cabinet doors, tile, and countertops.

9 engineered wood

10 stone

3 new paints They are easier to keep clean and some new types bond to all sorts of surfaces, including plastic laminate.

4 ceramic tile
- a classic choice
- lots of colors, patterns
- relatively easy to install
- many price points
- easy to maintain
- uses: floors, backsplashes, counters

5 concrete It's versatile and can be tinted, textured, and formed into interesting shapes.

6 quartz composite This nonporous, nonabsorbent surfacing material is 93 percent natural quartz; the rest is resin fillers. It is resistant to mold and mildew, scratches, stains, cracks, heat, and most household chemicals.

7 metal
- a trend that's here for the long run
- includes stainless steel and copper
- goes with any decorating style
- some finishes repel fingerprints

8 solid surfacing
- durable
- many colors and patterns
- relatively easy to maintain

- sometimes available with built-in antibacterial protection
- moldable

9 engineered wood
- looks like real wood
- available in many finishes
- relatively easy to install
- easy to maintain

10 stone
- available as tiles or slabs
- many types endure all kinds of abuse
- relatively easy to maintain
- goes with any style

Countertops and Backsplashes

Popular choices today include stone, quartz composite, solid-surfacing material, concrete, ceramic tile, wood, and stainless steel, although standard plastic laminate is an option.

If your counter area is small, you're probably safe staying with one type of material. Otherwise, think about matching the material to the task—a marble insert for a bake center or butcher block on an island where you chop vegetables, for example. Remember: some materials such as stone need more maintenance than others. Finally, don't leave the backsplash naked; choose to match or use another material there.

Granite Is Still Numero Uno, but...

On "those" TV shows, everybody "has to have" granite countertops. Granted, this stone is still the most popular choice for a countertop—it's a classic, after all—but quartz composite is right behind it on the charts and is climbing fast. (See page 90.)

Granite has its virtues. It's beautiful, hard as a diamond and, unlike marble, it's practically nonporous; you can slice and dice on it, and dough won't stick to it. Still, you will have to seal it periodically.

There are other stone choices, though they may not be as popular as granite. Marble is equally fetching, but it's delicate. Limestone and slate are less elegant, but they are durable and have a rustic appeal. And, of course, because they are natural stone, they require periodic sealing to keep stains from marring their looks.

You have a choice of edge treatments with stone. Notice the elegance of this marble countertop, opposite left, with an ogee edge. The subtle pattern of this coffee-toned polished granite, center, plays beautifully with the custom mosaic-tile backsplash. Slate, above, can be honed to create a smooth surface.

Quartz Composite

Quartz-composite material (often referred to simply as "quartz") is relatively new to the market. It offers the best of both worlds—the beauty and durability of natural stone and the easy maintenance of a laminate.

Composite material is produced by binding stone chips (typically quartz) to powders and resins to form an extremely durable product. Its textured and variegated look resembles stone, but the patterns formed are more consistent; patterns found in natural stone are random. Quartz comes in more colors, too.

This material also has practical virtues. It cleans easily and is heat and scratch resistant. Because it is nonporous, it doesn't need to be sealed or polished for it to resist stains and retain its finish. You can use it alone or for an integral sink and countertop application. Price-wise, quartz-composite material is comparable to natural stone in most cases.

Quartz-composite material offers versatility. Subtle silvery flecks in this almost entirely black example, above, make it understatedly elegant. This owner of this sleek kitchen, opposite and bottom, chose a polished pure white. There are other finishes and colors—and quartz's uniformity offers many treatment possibilities.

This curved counter, above, looks like granite, but it's actually fabricated from a solid-surface material.

Practical Synthetics

Solid color-through surfacing material is an extremely durable, easily maintained synthetic made of polyester or acrylic. It's expensive, costing almost as much per linear foot as natural stone, but it wears long and well. The material is impervious to water, and you can repair any dents or abrasions with a light sanding. You can use it on the counter-top and backsplash or for an integral sink and countertop application. Some types come with built-in antibacterial protection.

Standard plastic laminate, on the other hand, is made of several layers of melamine, paper, and plastic resin that are bonded under heat and pressure and then glued to par-ticleboard or plywood. Unlike solid-surfacing material, it's inexpensive, relatively easy to install, and available in a vast array of colors and some textures. Lesser grades will chip and crack, so don't skimp.

Some solid-surface materials, above and right, have a built-in antibacterial agent.

This bamboo parquet butcher-block countertop, top left, and traditional bamboo countertop, bottom left, have been made with a formaldehyde-free food-safe adhesive. A traditional hardwood countertop, below, wears a handsome, deep-walnut color.

Wood, a Natural Beauty

Wood is unrivaled for its natural warmth and beauty. Some cooks even love it when it starts to stain and show scratches. But wood may warp if exposed to water, so you'll have to seal it with a film finish of varnish or lacquer. To maintain it, make sure to sand and reseal it every year. If you cut directly on your countertop, treat it with nontoxic mineral oil, instead.

Teak is an excellent choice. So is eco-friendly bamboo, which is actually a grass but can substitute for wood. Both of these materials wear well and hold up against moisture.

Butcher block, a laminated wood product, is another countertop option. Eastern hard rock sugar maple is the best for use in butcher block; it resists scratches, warping, and uneven wearing.

Earth-Friendly Recycled Glass

If you want to go green, consider a recycled-glass countertop. This sturdy, solid surface is made of crushed recycled glass with a concrete binding and then sealed. In addition to doing something for the planet with your choice, you'll be reaping the benefits of a luminous surface that is not only different—in a good way—but more affordable than stone. Heat resistant and hygienic, a recycled-glass countertop will hold up against stains and scratches as long as you reseal it every two to three months. This basically involves simply coating the surface with one of several products that you can buy in the store.

Glass countertops tend to look slick and modern, but they work with traditional kitchens as well. You can find the material prefabricated or have it custom designed.

go green

GLASS WITH CLASS

If you haven't started to do it yet, get with the program and recycle your glass bottles and jars. Besides, it's great to know that some of the most beautiful ones—in cobalt blue, warm amber, and deep green, in particular—might be part of a gorgeous glass countertop one day.

This countertop has been made from 100-percent recycled glass and cement. It is manufactured in slabs and requires a professional installer who has knowledge of the product.

do this... not that

soak it up and then some

In addition to harsh or acid-based chemicals, vinegar, wine, and even cola can stain or etch a glass countertop. But accidents happen, and so after wiping up the liquid, reapply sealer to the counter surface. And whenever you notice that water doesn't bead up on it, that's a sign that it's time to reseal the countertop.

You can use a bullnose (half or full), pencil, or eased edge on a glass countertop. Ask your fabricator to show you samples.

Pearl-gray is another example of what you can find in a glass countertop palette, but there are vivid colors from which to choose, too. Look online for sources.

An outstanding feature in this kitchen is the exquisite stone and rich wood used for the countertops and backsplash. Marble is incomparable for its elegance. If you love it, but you need something that is more spill and stain tolerant, choose a granite with veining. **Far right:** Here, the creamy-white tones in the stone blend beautifully with the color of the cabinets. **Top right:** A gorgeous redwood on one counter warms up the all-white room.

it's in the
details ✳

Middle right: See how the wood picks up tones in the stone's veins. **Bottom right:** You can remove the lid and brush crumbs and scraps right into a composting bin.

surfaces

Concrete and Stainless Steel

These two industrial materials have found their way into residential kitchens. Once considered too cold for most tastes, concrete and stainless steel, in the hands of a talented designer, pose no threat to coziness.

Concrete is quite versatile, can be formed into any number of shapes and is a natural choice for an integral sink-and-counter installation. It can look equally at home in a minimalist or a rustic kitchen.

You can color concrete or leave it natural, but you must seal it. However, concrete is resistant to heat and scratching. Use it near the cooktop as a landing for hot pots. Although concrete is not expensive, the fabrication can take time, and you will pay accordingly.

Stainless steel is practically ubiquitous in residential kitchens thanks to the still-strong popularity of professional-style appliances. Interest in the material has carried over to countertops and backsplashes, something only seen in commercial kitchens in the past. On the plus side, it's extremely durable, hygienic, and impervious to heat and stains. It can be formed into an integral sink-and-countertop configuration, and satin and brushed finishes will hide scratches. On the down side, it's expensive and can be noisy.

This polished-concrete countertop, opposite, would look at home with any architectural style.
It's strong but not as heavy as granite or marble. One of the most hygienic surfaces you can choose
is stainless steel, above.

Tile

When you can't afford a countertop fabricated from a stone slab, **stone tile** is the answer. There may be limited color offerings, but you can find granite tile that's suitable for a countertop or backsplash, for example, in a home-improvement store.

When you think of tile, though, **ceramic tile** usually comes to mind. There are even versions that look like metal and stone. Glazed ceramic tile is impervious to water, so it is perfect near the sink. It is also durable and will not scratch, burn, or stain. Aside from its practical attributes, ceramic tile offers the greatest opportunity for adding color, pattern, and texture to your kitchen, particularly on a backsplash.

Luminous **glass tile** may be too delicate for a kitchen countertop, but it is a dressy choice for a backsplash as a solid or a mosaic design—or as an accent.

Plan something special for your backsplash. Ceramic tiles are a smart choice because anything that splashes on them wipes off easily. Design an interesting pattern for a custom look.

do this... not that

you can fake it

If splurging on a granite countertop puts a dent in your budget, you can still finish your backsplash with a flourish. Ceramic tile that looks like stone is the answer. Look for a color that coordinates with the countertop. Keep the field tiles simple, and add a decorative touch here and there with accent tiles or with a border. For added interest, look for rope borders or raised (relief) patterns.

This attractive backsplash features affordable 2 x 2-in. tiles that can be found in any home-improvement store. The accent pieces add a special touch.

Glass tile, particularly mosaics in iridescent finishes, bring bling into any cooking space. **Far right:** Glass tiles are delicate, and so it's smart to reserve them for an application on the wall. Here's a perfect example of how to use them to their best advantage.

Top right: This homeowner created drama by extending the glass-tile backsplash all the way to the top of the wall behind the cooktop. It's perfect paired with the stainless-steel hood.

it's in the
details ✱

Bottom right: The undercabinet lighting makes the tiles shimmer. You can also see them reflected in the glass cabinet fronts and on the stone countertop.

STEP 1 weigh your options

If you are sprucing up an old kitchen or adding a new one in a house you expect to sell soon, you might install a less-expensive countertop material. But if you are making a major investment in a remodeling project that you plan to live with for a long time, you will be happier in the long run with materials that may cost more but will give you satisfaction for years to come.

A countertop or a floor is not that difficult to change if you are unhappy with your choice as time passes. But unless you are able to do the work yourself, making such changes will cost money.

STEP 2 prorate costs

You may be dismayed by the price of some types of materials, but when you divide the cost of the product by its anticipated longevity (how many years you expect it to last), you may be amazed at how reasonable the price is. Of course, this won't alleviate an immediate cash-flow problem, but it will ease some of the sticker shock. An expensive product that will last for 20 years may be a better choice than a cheaper one that may have to be replaced in 5 years. Again, weigh that decision against how long you plan to stay in the house. Are the extra benefits worth spending the extra money?

Smart Flooring Choices

Flooring plays a style role in your kitchen, but it affects function, too. Generally, materials that are hard, such as stone or ceramic tile, may be uncomfortable to stand on for long periods of time. Still, many people choose them because they last forever, and they are exceptionally handsome.

Solid wood, engineered wood, and wood laminates, however, are more flexible and thus more comfortable underfoot for extended periods of time. Engineered wood and wood look-alikes in laminate (the least costly) are the most practical of the three, requiring little care. If you must have solid wood, be prepared—you can't scrub it; it's expensive; and even the hardwoods are far from indestructible.

Cushiony vinyl and other resilient flooring is the most economical option. The best quality will last for decades.

Bamboo is very comfortable underfoot, above. The family pooch agrees, left. But tile is still popular because it needs little care. Diamond shapes dress up plain ceramic tiles, opposite top. Slate tiles, opposite bottom, add a rustic touch to a country kitchen.

go green

BAMBOO

Because it replenishes itself so quickly, bamboo is an eco-friendly material. It's available in two basic grain patterns, horizontal and vertical; the latter is better for damp locations. If you buy prefinished bamboo planks, look for a healthy low volatile organic compound (VOC) rating.

My old kitchen has carpeting. I'm planning to remodel. I need something on the floor, but not vinyl or linoleum. Any suggestions?

what the experts say

Most experts don't recommend carpeting in a kitchen. It's simply impractical in a room where spills and greasy stains occur frequently, although some types of carpet are treated for stain and wear resistance.

A natural option to consider is cork. It's comfortable and wears well in a high-traffic area, such as a kitchen. In fact, according to the Cork Industry of America, "No other material recovers from compression or puncture like cork."

what real people do

Homeowners looking for a natural alternative to manufactured flooring, such as resilient vinyl, find that cork is a smart choice. It's not only beautiful but sustainable.

Cork comes in the form of preglued and prefinished tiles or floating-floor panels and in different colors. A cork floor is not difficult to install, making it a good project for the do-it-yourselfer.

If ceramic tile or stone is too cold and hard, consider a faux look in resilient vinyl, left and below. A wood laminate floor, opposite bottom, costs less than the real thing, but it looks great and is easy to maintain.

Ceiling Treatments

The fifth wall—the ceiling—is begging for attention. Sure, you could paint it white and leave it at that, but why? Ceilings offer a blank canvas where you can add architectural interest. Ideas include a tray-style ceiling, molding, paneling, beams, tin panels, a lighted cove, or a textural treatment.

Keep the style of your home in mind when you're choosing a ceiling treatment. For example, bead-board paneling looks great in a cottage-style or country kitchen, and wood beams can lend Old World charm to a traditional design.

To honor the past, the designer paneled the walls and ceiling in this renovated kitchen, left, in an older home. Painted beams, inset, finish the look, adding architectural character in keeping with the rest of the house.

A textured ceiling with wood beams, right, is a great look for an Old World country kitchen. In this contemporary design, opposite bottom, a circular recess with lights becomes the focal point.

water works

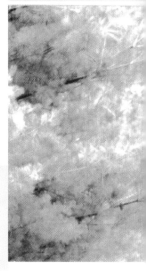

Kitchen sinks and faucets—what could be more basic? Actually, there's nothing basic about them today. Sophisticated engineering and top-notch design make them heavy hitters performance- and style-wise. Whether you are a home gourmet or someone who likes to keep meals simple, you'll appreciate what today's kitchen sinks and faucets have to offer—however much or little you want to spend.

Buying a kitchen sink involves choosing a style, material, and bowl size. Then you'll need the right faucet.

Super Bowls

Nowadays, kitchens often have two sinks; the primary sink anchors the main food preparation and cleanup areas, while a smaller secondary sink serves outside of the major work zone.

In terms of installation, there are six types of sinks to consider for your kitchen.

Under-mounted. The bowl is attached underneath the countertop.

Integral. The sink and countertop are fabricated from the same solid block of material.

Exposed apron. This type of under-mount reveals the sink's front panel.

Rimmed. A flat metal strip seals the bowl to the countertop.

Self-rimming or drop-in. An attached rolled-edge rim secures the sink to the countertop.

Tiled-in. Used with a tiled countertop, the rim of the bowl is flush with the tiled surface. Grout seals the sink to the surrounding countertop area.

For the most part, all of these types of installations will work with almost any kitchen, depending on the material, the finish, and the style of the faucet.

A farmhouse sink, below left, is a favorite in cottage kitchens. It's typically under-mounted, but sometimes it can be a tiled-in installation. A trough sink, below, may be under-mounted or integrated with the countertop.

A retro-style sink with an integrated backsplash, above, can be dropped into a countertop or mounted on the wall. Stainless steel, stone, concrete, and solid-surfacing material, right, are suitable for an integral sink and countertop.

One Size Does Not Fit All

Two- and three-bowl configurations are practical, especially if there isn't a secondary sink in a separate work zone. This arrangement allows you to separate clean dishes from dirty ones and waste materials. Some sinks come with a colander and cutting board. A waste-disposal unit is typically installed with one of the bowls, usually the larger one. Just peel your potatoes; then whisk the skins down the drain. Lay the cutting board over the top of the bowl for chopping, and afterwards push the potato slices into the colander for rinsing.

A triple-bowl kitchen sink, right, may be a good idea in a busy kitchen that does not have the physical space to spare for a second sink.

Standard Sink Sizes

SINK DIMENSIONS (in inches)

Sink Type	Width	Front to Rear	Basin Depth
Single-bowl	25	21–22	8–9
Double-bowl	33, 36	21–22	8–9
Side-disposal	33	21–22	8–9, 7
Triple-bowl	43	21–22	8, 6, 10
Corner	17–18	21–11 (each way)	8–9
Bar	15–25	15	5½–6

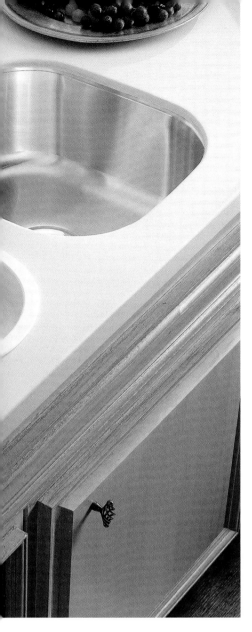

For this double-sink corner installation to be efficient, above right, the faucet must have a wide swivel range that's adequate to serve both bowls. A double-bowl sink, right, is handy for separately washing and rinsing.

One Size Does Not Fit All **119**

It's a Material World

You have choices. Today's kitchen sinks may be fabricated from enameled cast iron, stainless steel, copper, solid stone, a composite material (solid-surfacing, acrylic, or a mixture of natural quartz with resins), or concrete. They may be hand-painted or decorated with silk-screened designs, contoured, beveled, brushed to a matte finish, or polished to a mirror finish.

In terms of durability, any one of the materials mentioned above will hold up well for years, if not decades, with the right care. Enameled cast-iron sinks tend to discolor but can be cleaned easily with a nonabrasive cleanser. Stainless steel, copper, stone, and concrete should be cleaned the same way. However, composite sinks are scratch resistant, with the exception of inexpensive acrylic models, so you can use an abrasive agent on them if necessary.

You can expect a good-quality kitchen sink to last as long as 30 years.

A stainless-steel sink, top right, is a popular choice, and it looks good with any countertop material. A sink made from a composite material, middle right, may come in a wide variety of colors. You can also have a sink that is made from the same material as your countertop. This one, bottom right, is soapstone. Sinks made of vitreous china, opposite, have a durable, glossy finish.

2 commercial-style

4 pot fillers

the top **10**

Sink & Faucet Ideas

1 **stainless steel** This is the most popular material chosen for kitchen sinks today. It looks good with both professional-style and standard appliances. But be careful, stainless steel comes in different grades. Inferior qualities can scratch easily, may be noisy, and can sound tinny.

2 **commercial-style faucets** Inspired by the popularity of professional-style appliances and today's cooking trends, including the home gourmet, these upscale faucets feature advanced engineering and bring another level of restaurant efficiency into the home. Features include a pull-down spout, a flexible hose, and easy operation with touch-control technology.

7 exposed aprons

9 water stations

3 under-mounted sinks This type of sink installation looks sleek and avoids the seams that catch food particles and harbor germs.

4 pot fillers Faucets installed over the cooktop eliminate the chore of carrying water from the sink to the burner. Some are fixed, while others have an articulated arm that reaches across all of the burners.

5 water filtration For people who are concerned about the quality of their tap water, there are faucets that come with a built-in filtration system.

6 euro styling Modern European designs have strong geometric lines, such as L-shaped spouts and cylindrical levers.

7 exposed aprons Sinks with an exposed apron, also called "farmhouse sinks," appeal to those with a love of all things retro as well as contemporary tastes.

8 accessories Sink accessories, such as soap and lotion dispensers, separate sprayers, and instant-hot-water tap, are often sold as matching sets with faucets.

9 water stations These fully equipped kitchen islands are considered multipurpose work stations. They are connected to the kitchen plumbing and incorporate a sink, cutting boards, and a waste-disposal unit.

10 pullouts, pull downs, and telescopic faucets These faucets bring the water to you or where you need it, making pot filling and cleanup tasks easier.

Faucets & Fittings

Sleek European-inspired designs and commercial styles are the big news in kitchen faucets. Today's models bring beauty and function into your kitchen with innovative technology that gives you more control over water use and better, longer-lasting finishes. Features to look for include pullout faucet heads, retractable sprayers, single-lever control, anti-scald and flow-control devices, a lead content lower than 0.25 percent, and built-in water purifiers.

For a quality faucet, the best are those made of solid brass, a brass-base material, or solid stainless steel. All are corrosion-resistant. Avoid plastic components—they won't hold up. Ask about valving, too. Ball valves are good for single-lever faucets; ceramic-disk cartridges may be used in single- and dual-lever faucets. Washerless valving will cost more, but the faucet will last longer and be less prone to leaks.

A high-arching spout and a drop-down spray with a flexible hose, opposite, offer ease of use and functionality. This pretty, oiled-bronze design, above, was designed for a bar sink. This single-lever mixer, below, has a pullout sprayer and comes in a brushed-nickel finish.

More Features

Spouts and levers in attractive shapes and finishes that coordinate with your sink can put a finishing touch on your kitchen's style.

A pullout faucet, as opposed to one that is stationary or only swivels side to side, offers the greatest flexibility. It's convenient for washing tall pots and pans, especially in a shallow sink. Some also come with a built-in sprayer.

Among the many types of handle styles, you'll find wrist blades, levers, scrolls, geometric shapes, and cross handles.

Nickel, chrome, stainless-steel, copper, and bronze finishes are popular, and polished and brushed gold has recently been introduced into the market. Technologically advanced coatings can make even delicate finishes more durable unless you use abrasive cleansers on them.

This widespread design in rubbed bronze, right, matches the separate sprayer and a soap dispenser. A filtered hot-water dispenser is a handy accessory to the single-lever mixer, opposite.

do this... not that

buying a faucet? think sink

When you are buying a kitchen faucet, make sure it suits the sink, not just in style but in terms of function as well. For example, if your sink has a shallow bowl, choose a pullout rather than a stationary faucet. This will make washing large bowls and deep pots easier. Also, a faucet with a high-arc spout will cause splashing unless you use it with a sink that has a deep bowl.

Another thing to consider is whether the spout is the right type for the size of the sink. If it's a double- or triple-bowl sink, make sure that the faucet's swivel range is adequate. The spout should reach the center of each bowl.

This flush-mounted horizontal fixed spout, right, is suitable for a second sink that is reserved for rinsing fruit or vegetables.

For this homeowner, who entertains on a large scale, there is no such thing as too many cooks in the kitchen or too many kitchen sinks.

Far right: You can see access to water at various stations, or zones, in this layout—at the island, above the cooktop, and at the cleanup area against the wall with the windows.

Top right: The bridge-style faucet complements the kitchen's traditional details.

it's in the
details ✳

Bottom right: A beverage center is located in another part of the large room. The copper sink and faucet **(inset)** coordinates with the dark cabinetry and wood countertop.

Convenience on Tap

Gourmets and anyone who does a lot of cooking will appreciate the new commericial-style faucets that bring restaurant efficiency into the home kitchen today. These include faucets with telescopic spouts that pull out, bringing the water to you; faucets with pull-down wands and flexible hoses for easy rinsing; faucets with extra-wide swivel ranges; and touch technology that allows you to turn on or turn off the faucet with a light tap using your forearm or elbow, keeping the handle away from potential contaminants on your hands. Finally, there's pot fillers—faucets that are installed on the wall above the cooktop. Those with articulated arms offer the most convenience.

go green

KEEP THE FLOW LOW

Buy a faucet with a flow rate of 2.2 gallons per minute or less. Most new faucets have a built-in flow-control device that mixes air into the stream, cutting usage without affecting water pressure.

This commericial-inspired design with cylindical levers, left, has a drop-down sprayer. Strong lines give this single-hole faucet, below, an ultra-modern look. Matching accessories include a soap/lotion dispenser, a filtered-water dispenser, and a separate sprayer.

A swivel-arm pot-filler faucet is a convenience some pasta cooks can't live without.

STEP 1 weigh the options

Compare the advantages and any disadvantages of choosing one type of sink or faucet over another. Things to consider include:

■ **Cost.** For many people, this is the deciding factor. In that case, you need to know that a hand-painted china sink will be expensive, and it may not pay back at resale time. In most cases, a synthetic material is more affordable.

■ **Care.** Okay, so you can afford to splurge on a black granite sink. But hard-water stains must be treated immediately. Once again, an easy-care synthetic material is a practical alternative.

STEP 2 look for bargains?

Shop around to get the best price. Visit several stores and showrooms and look online. Be careful, however; there may be a good reason why two seemingly identical faucets or sinks are priced differently. It may be about

■ **Quality.** It's easy to find products today that look upscale but are sold at bargain-basement prices. That's why you should never choose a product based solely on looks. Buy the best quality you can afford.

■ **Brand.** You might pay more for a well-known brand. But usually the manufacturer has earned its high reputation and will honor its warranties.

STEP 3 be eco-friendly

Buy a faucet with an aerater that has a flow rate of 2.2 gallons per minute or less. Or even better, look for a faucet that comes with a WaterSense label.

Initiated by the Environmental Protection Agency (EPA), the WaterSense program sets up stringent standards backed up by independent testing and certification. The program was established to ensure that a product, such as a faucet, is manufactured to be water efficient without compromising its performance. WaterSense-labeled faucets are 20 percent more efficient than their standard counterparts.

STEP 4 filter—if necessary

Your tap water is probably perfectly safe. But if you are worried about pollutants that might be in the water system, contact your local health department and ask for a list of water contaminants in your area.

If you decide that you need a filtering system, you can buy either one that comes with the faucet or one that you can have installed under the sink or on the counter. Check to see whether the water filter has been certified by the National Sanitation Foundation, a non-profit testing lab, for efficiency in removing contaminants. Go to the foundation's Web site: www.nsf.org.

appliances

Next to the cabinets, new appliances will likely be the largest investment you'll make in your new kitchen. The best thing to do is to check out all of the options and styles on the market and choose appliances that best serve the size of your household, your cooking style, and the types of foods you like to eat. If cooking and preparing food is your passion, you'll appreciate the features included in many of today's top-of-the-line models.

There are appliances on the market that cater to all budgets and lifestyles. You can also customize your cooking and refrigeration systems.

Now You're Cookin'

There are a few basic questions you'll have to answer up front about your cooking equipment. What kind of fuel will it use, gas or electric? Will it be a configuration of a separate cooktop and ovens or will they be contained in one unit? Will you combine fuels in the same appliance?

If you can't make up your mind about fuel, you should at least know that the type you select makes a difference. Most professional chefs and gourmets recommend gas burners for precise heat control and electric or convection ovens for even heat.

Should you install a range or a separate cooktop and ovens? The range is a smart choice if you have limited space. It may also be the most economical option because you won't incur the cost of multiple hookups and additional ventilation. However, separate cooktops and wall ovens conveniently allow you to customize the work centers and install them where they fit best into the traffic pattern and work flow. This arrangement is ideal in a kitchen with multiple cooks. Modular units in some models can be tailored to the way you cook. Besides two-, four-, five-, six-, or eight-burner units, you can purchase accessories—built-in units, such as a deep fryer or a steamer, or detachable, interchangeable parts that give you greater cooking flexibility and make cleanup easier.

Freestanding ranges may incorporate more than one oven. This professional-style model, below left, also has an interchangeable grill and griddle. Stainless steel is popular, but you can also find a range with color, such as this one, below. If you prefer to keep ovens separate, a cooktop, opposite, can give you design flexibility.

Some cooking systems can be customized to your cooking style and needs. **Far right:** This dual-fuel cooking station features a high-output gas burner, a steamer, and an electric cooktop. **Top right:** On the kitchen island (not pictured), there's a "mini hub" that has a two-burner electric

it's in the
details ✳

cooktop and a built-in steamer. **Middle right:** A high-heat gas burner can be used for wok cooking or for searing meat. **Bottom right:** Another option for this kitchen could be a combination of a deep fryer, a grill, and gas burners.

Gas versus Electric

You can adjust the flame and cook more evenly on a gas burner. Many models now come with electronic ignition (no worrisome pilot lights).

If you prefer an electric cooktop, there is the traditional type with **coil elements** that heat quickly but take time cooling; you can't go from sizzle to simmer instantly. Then there are those that have heating elements under a ceramic-glass top. **Radiant-heat** cooktops have electric-resistance coils under the translucent glass that transfer heat efficiently to cookware. **Halogen** cooktops use halogen lamps to heat the cooking surface. **Induction** cooktops use electromagnetic energy to heat the cookware, not the cooktop. You can adjust the heat as precisely and as quickly as you would with gas burners, but you usually must use magnetic-responsive cookware—steel, porcelain on steel, stainless steel, or cast iron.

No heat is generated by a flame or a coil on an induction cooktop, opposite. And because only the cookware gets hot, spills won't burn, making cleanup easy. A "speed oven," top left, combines microwave and convection technology to cook up to eight times faster than a conventional gas oven. A popular space-saving arrangement is a range with an over-the-range microwave/lighting/venting system, left.

go green

UNWASTED ENERGY

Almost all of the energy—85 percent—supplied by an induction cooktop goes directly to the cooking vessel. By comparison, less than half that amount—40 percent—of the energy in gas gets used to cook.

Clothes may make the man (or woman), as the saying goes, but smart appliances make the kitchen. **Far right:** A-list appliances transform this kitchen into a gourmet's dream, starting with a restaurant-style gas range with a built-in convection oven. **Top right:** This bottom-mount refrigerator freezer fits snugly into the space next to a cabinet. Its extra width compensates for its shallower-than-standard depth. **Bottom right:** This microwave drawer is

it's in the details *

also installed to fit flush into the end of the island. Its location allows for heating snacks away from the main cooking zone.

find pro-style appliances
@ www.wolf.com
www.dacor.com

Venting

The only thoroughly efficient way to combat the stale air that lingers after cooking is with a **hooded** exhaust system. A fan over the range or cooktop is not enough. The hood, which is installed directly over the cooking surface, captures the bad air and moisture vapor as it heats and naturally rises. A fan expels the contaminants to the outside through a duct. A damper inside the hood closes when the system is turned off so that cold air can't enter the house from the outside. Don't try to save money by installing a ductless fan: any system that isn't ducted to the outside is useless.

Sizing Ventilation Fans

No matter how attractive a hood may be, it is the fan in the system that actually takes the air out of the kitchen. Fans are sized by the amount of air they can move in cubic feet per minute (CFM). Here are some guidelines to help you size the ventilation fan for your needs: multiply the recommended CFM below by the linear feet of cooking surface. Note: the length of the duct-work, the number of turns in the duct, and the location of the fan's motor also contribute to the size of the fan needed.

RANGES AND COOKTOPS
installed against a wall:

Light Cooking: 40 CFM

Medium to Heavy Cooking: 100 to 150 CFM

RANGES AND COOKTOPS
installed in islands and peninsulas:

Light Cooking: 50 CFM

Medium to Heavy Cooking: 150 to 300 CFM

Down-draft ventilation, which is installed with an island cooktop, top, forces the air above the burners through a filter and then moves it out of the house via ductwork that runs under the floor to the outdoors. A professional-style range, above, requires a large hood and powerful ventilation.

A paneled exhaust hood becomes integrated with the cabinetry with similar molding and decorative paneling.

Keepin' It Cool

Refrigeration has gone way beyond the basic box. Now it comes in different sizes, shapes, and configurations for added convenience.

Conventional wisdom recommends allocating 12 cubic feet for two people in a household and another 2 cubic feet for each additional person. Increase the total by another 2 cubic feet if you entertain often. That's the formula, but not all lifestyles fit into it. If you shop in bulk, you may need more; if you eat out often, you may need less. So consider your unique habits and needs.

Refrigerator sizes vary by more than capacity. Traditionally, units have protruded beyond the full depth of a base cabinet. As kitchen design has become sleeker, manufacturers have responded with 24-inch-

A few high-end manufacturers make refrigerator and freezer columns, left, with no visible grilles or hinges so that they blend into the cabinets. Along with modular drawers, below, for chilling or freezing foods, they can be paired in different configurations and with full-size units for greater design options. A French-door style, opposite, and other bottom-freezer models put refrigerated foods at eye level.

deep models that fit snugly into a corresponding-size opening in a run of cabinetry for a built-in appearance. But as refrigerators have become shallower, they have also become wider to make up for lost storage capacity. Width varies greatly, so check the appliance's spec sheet when you're allocating space in your layout.

There are several general refrigerator styles. A **top-mount** has a freezer compartment on the top that is separate from the refrigerator compartment.

A **bottom-freezer configuration** locates a separate freezer compartment below the refrigerator.

A **side-by-side refrigerator/freezer** offers the greatest access to both compartments and requires the least door-swing clearance in front.

A **French-door model** has two refrigerator doors that open in the center and a freezer below.

2 integrated appliances

4 microwave drawer

6 French doors

the top 10

Hot and Cool Appliance Trends

1 professional cooking The features offered with cooking appliances for today's at-home gourmet rival some restaurants. They include built-in fryers and steamers; grills and griddles; commercial-style broilers; and high-heat burners for charring and precise low-heat for simmering.

2 integrated appliances Although stainless steel doesn't seem to have lost any popularity, some homeowners choose custom cabinet fronts and panels that blend their appliances with their kitchen cabinetry for a totally coordinated look.

7 shallow depth

9 induction cooking

3 **speed** Speed-cooking appliances combine microwave, convection, and air-assisted technologies that let you roast a chicken in 25 minutes.

4 **appliance drawers** Modular appliances can save space, and they make ergonomic sense, eliminating the need to bend in some cases. They include
- refrigerators
- freezers
- dishwashers
- microwaves

5 **steam** The trend toward healthier eating has inspired appliance manufacturers to create built-in steaming units for the home cook.

6 **French doors** This practically walk-in style of refrigeration owes as much to its looks as it does to its handy eye-level reach-in appeal.

7 **shallow depth** To make a seamless line in a run of cabinets interrupted by an appliance, shallow, 24-inch-deep units come to the rescue.

8 **hip hoods** Decorative canopies created to camouflage hooded ventilation systems can be custom made, although some cabinet manufacturers make them to match their cabinets.

9 **induction cooking** These cool-to-the-touch cooktops are energy efficient, and some models no longer require using special cookware.

10 **wine coolers** Midrange models have made this "luxury item" more affordable for homeowners.

Dishwashers

New dishwashers are more energy efficient, use less water, and are quieter today. Ones with a stainless-steel interior, which will cost more, can take the beating of dishwashing chemicals and high heat on a daily basis. It will last twice as long as other dishwashers, and so the higher price may be worth it. Another optional feature that may interest you is convection drying, which uses a built-in fan to air-dry dishes instead of the energy-consuming heat cycle. For more energy savings, some dishwashers have an internal heating device, so you can turn down the setting on your water heater. You can also find modular units, called "dish drawers," that you can use alone just for glassware in a beverage center, in pairs to wash different types of items, or as a supplement to a full-size model.

An elevated dishwasher, above, is desirable if you don't want to bend to load and unload it. The best location for a dishwasher is next to the sink, right.

do this... not that

comparing models

Most dishwashers come with three cycles for light, normal, and heavy cleaning and cost about $500. Before you spend $1,500 on a fancy model, decide whether you need these price-boosting features: a dirt sensor; rinse/hold cycle; special wash cycles for china and crystal and pots and pans; steam cleaning; and sanitizing.

With dishwasher drawers, below, you can do smaller loads and separate items such as pots and pans from dishes and glassware.

Q + A

I don't want to bend over to load dishes. But dishwasher drawers are small, and stacking two means the one on the bottom will be too low. Help!

what the experts say

"You have two options that will allow you to load a dishwasher without bending over," suggest the experts at the National Kitchen and Bath Association (NKBA). "Place a single dishwasher drawer on each side of the sink. The second is to elevate a standard dishwasher." (See page 150.) Many people prefer an elevated dishwasher, and some cabinet manufacturers have responded by making a 27- x 42-inch cabinet that "lifts the appliance off the floor. The box is finished on each side similar to a base cabinet."

what real people do

You can ask your contractor to build a box that will lift up your dishwasher. Your cabinet dealer should be able to provide materials to match the sides of your other cabinetry. However, the NKBA cautions, "Normally, we suggest placing the dishwasher next to the sink. However, elevating a dishwasher can cause a problem [as it will elevate the counter height]." In that case, the NKBA says to "move the dishwasher away from the sink by no more than 36 inches from the [side] edge of the sink rim to the [side] edge of the dishwasher. This works well if the dishwasher is next to a tall cabinet or the refrigerator."

Thoughtful placement of your appliances will improve your kitchen's efficiency.

What Not to Forget

You may also want to include small but handy appliances such as a waste-disposal unit. Check with your building department; some communities require them or a specific type; others ban them. If you live in a community that charges by the bag for removing garbage, you'll appreciate the savings a trash compactor may offer. Some models stand alone, but you can incorporate a compactor that is built in and finished to match the cabinetry.

And as coffee drinking has become so popular, so have built-in coffee stations. Several manufacturers offer this appliance, which requires plumbing.

For a beverage center, especially if you do a lot of entertaining, you'll want to check out a wine cooler, an under-counter refrigerator, and an ice maker.

A beverage center can keep guests happy and out of the kitchen work zone. Include an under-cabinet refrigerator, top, to hold cold drinks and a handy ice maker, left. This coffee station, above, is plumbed. A wine cooler can fit neatly under the counter, opposite, or reach the top of the cabinets.

STEP 1 think ahead

Will the refrigerator you purchase now serve you adequately for the next dozen years? Do you intend to be cooking more or less? If you anticipate that your household will increase or decrease in size within the next few years, you may want to reevaluate the size of any new appliance models you plan to purchase and upgrade or downgrade accordingly.

You might also want to reevaluate your choices in terms of resale value. Professional appliances may be high on your wish list, but don't expect a return on your investment.

STEP 2 note efficiency

Manufacturers are required by law to label every appliance with certain energy-related information. That information must include a description of the appliance, the model number, projected energy costs to run the appliance, a range of energy costs for similar models, and a table to estimate energy costs for running the appliance based on local utility rates.

Look for the Energy Star label, which indicates that an appliance meets standards set by the Environmental Protection Agency (EPA). Such qualified appliances use 10 to 50 percent less energy than standard appliances.

STEP 3 make sure it fits

Don't find out after the appliance has been delivered that it's too wide for its allocated location. Always check the measurements on your floor plan against the manufacturer's specifications and the actual in-store model. It always pays to bring a measuring tape to the store or showroom to check the floor models, too.

Another measurement to check is the depth of an appliance, especially if you want the look of something that is built-in. Some "cabinet-depth" refrigerators come 24 inches deep, for example, so that they are flush with the cabinetry for an integrated look.

STEP 4 look for easy care

You want to enjoy the new kitchen, but you won't if it's drudgery to keep it sparkling. Inquire about the finish and care—inside and out—of every appliance you purchase. For example, a stainless-steel finish on the exterior of an appliance tends to show fingerprints and smudges, but inside a refrigerator or dishwasher it's the most practical finish to keep clean. All it needs is an occasional sponging with water and a nonabrasive cleanser. And if you hate scrubbing an oven, it may be worth the extra amount (about $100) for one with a self-cleaning feature.

chapter 7
kitchen lighting

- ◆ NATURAL LIGHT
- ◆ IT'S IN THE DETAILS
- ◆ ARTIFICIAL LIGHT
- ◆ IT'S IN THE DETAILS
- ◆ LIGHTING FIXTURES
- ◆ IT'S IN THE DETAILS

Lighting technology has become rather sophisticated in recent times, and there's no other room in the house that can benefit from it more than the kitchen. In addition to always-desirable natural light, other sources of light are required for the various activities and general living that takes place in today's kitchen. Here are the basics for making your kitchen bright and welcoming.

A lighting plan that includes the various types of illumination will make your time in the kitchen comfortable, safe, and pleasant.

Natural Light

No real estate agent has ever heard a home-owner complain about too much natural light. With today's window technology, you can bring as much sunlight into your home as you like and at the same time depend on enhanced glazing options, such as low-E glass, to solve the problem of energy-inefficient windows.

On the style side, windows previously associated with custom designs, such as the "architectural" styles popular today, are now available in standard sizes. Replacing an uninspired window with a graceful arch-top design is relatively easy and affordable. In fact, it's not difficult to change the entire architectural look of your kitchen by replacing the windows. Want to transform a 50-year-old space into a stylish contemporary setting? Use sleek casement-style units. Looking for a way to add vintage character? Install double-hung windows with snap-in muntins that imitate true divided-light windows. Group individual casement or awning windows in an interesting formation along one wall. Where there is no place for a window, install an operable skylight, or roof window.

Giving up extra cabinets was no sacrifice for these homeowners, who wanted to flood their new kitchen with natural light, opposite. A roof window brightens the area near the range, above, which was once a dark corner in the kitchen pre-renovation.

The right details have been assembled to create a bright, efficient contemporary kitchen with a touch of nostalgia thrown into the mix. **Far right:** Retro-industrial-style pendants suspended over the center island punctuate the kitchen's turn-of-the-last-century twist. Their location, suitably high above the countertop, and their opaque-glass shades provide glare-free lighting at the island whether you're dining or seeing to a task.

it's in the
details ✳

Top right: The sliding window above the sink opens to a screened back porch.
Bottom right: Recessed canisters provide general lighting throughout.

Artificial Light

Artificial lighting is the easiest way to set or change the atmosphere of an entire room. With one switch, your kitchen can go from a bright, efficient hub of activity to a softly lit setting for a quiet meal. The right light can also make meal preparation and cleanup safer and more efficient. Think of how much time you might save if you could open a cabinet and spot whatever you need right away, or how quickly you could chop an onion in a bright, clear, shadowless space.

In addition, performing tasks that can feel like drudgery seem easier in the right light because your eyes are less susceptible to strain. The key

Including several types of fixture styles adds interest to this design, and polished-chrome pendants are a pleasing contrast to the white cabinets.

to devising a versatile plan that can change with each activity, as well as with the time of day, begins with knowing about the different types of artificial light. You'll need at least two types—**ambient,** or general, lighting and **task** lighting, but you should also include **accent** lighting in your plan. A fourth type, **decorative** lighting, is optional, but if you include it, you'll appreciate the effect it has on the way your kitchen looks.

If you think creating a plan for lighting your kitchen is too technical to do on your own, consult a lighting designer or in-store specialist.

This kitchen's layered lighting design includes accent lighting in the upper cabinets; undercabinet light strips illuminate work surfaces and draw attention to the beauty of the granite countertops, right. A reproduction pendant adds a formal note above the table, below.

Deep mellow wood tones and dark granite counters look rich in this transitional-style kitchen that combines elements of traditional and Modern design. **Far right:** A lighting design that brings out the warm tones in the wood and makes the stainless-steel appliances shimmer was a must. Daylight from the window floods the room with warm**th.**

Top right: Cylindrical hanging fixtures are spaced equidistantly in order to create an even spread of light over the counter.

it's in the details *

Bottom right: Accent lighting inside the cabinets picks up the fiery amber tones in the wood and looks decorative.

find Modern pendants
@ www.georgekovacs.com
www.lightology.com

kitchen lighting

General Lighting

Ambient, or general, lighting is illumination that fills an entire room. The source is sometimes an overhead fixture or a group of fixtures, but the light itself does not appear to come from any specific direction. The most obvious example is fluorescent strips; the covering over the strips hides the source and diffuses the light.

    The key to good ambient lighting is making it inconspicuous. It is merely the backdrop for the rest of the room, not the main feature. Ambient lighting used during the day should blend with the natural light that enters a room. During the evening, you should be able to diminish or soften the light level so that it doesn't contrast jarringly with the darkness outside.

Recessed canisters provide suitable general lighting for a kitchen if they are spaced properly.

go green

GO LIGHT
Energy-efficient compact fluorescent bulbs (CFLs) use about 75 percent less energy and last about 20 times longer than standard bulbs. Look for the Energy Star label.

Task Lighting

Task lighting is functional, illuminating specific areas for specific tasks, such as chopping vegetables, reading a recipe, or rolling out dough. It's essential for safety in a kitchen, especially when working around a hot stove or oven or using sharp instruments.

The key to good task lighting is installing it slightly to the side of each work surface. Small lights mounted to the underside of a cabinet are an excellent example of well-thought-out placement. If you placed the light sources directly overhead, your body would create shadows as you bend over the work surface.

do this...not that

glaring errors

Because kitchens contain so many surfaces that are highly reflective, be careful not to create glare with the lighting you choose.

One area of concern is the under-cabinet lighting designed to illuminate work areas on countertops. Make sure the lighting is shielded; never leave a bulb uncovered. Choose fixtures with opaque covers over the lamps. Install dimmers for maximum control.

Many vent hoods also come with lighting for the cooktop. In this case, above left, it also draws attention to a good-looking backsplash. Under-cabinet fixtures brighten a work area, above right.

A pendant can be decorative in addition to providing general or task lighting in a kitchen. Here, the wrought-iron finish on the fixture picks up the other black features in the room.

Q&A

Can I use a pendant over a downdraft cooktop? If that's not a good idea, is there another type of fixture I can use?

what the experts say

"The cooking center needs sufficient task lighting. With a downdraft vent, there is no need for a hood, which normally would have a light. The only option left is to use a hanging light," say the experts at the National Kitchen and Bath Association (NKBA).

There are two things to consider when using a pendant fixture this way: height and maintenance. The bottom of the fixture should be at least 30 inches above the cooktop. If you use downdraft venting properly, maintenance should not be a problem.

what real people do

Many homeowners install a pendant over an island that serves the dual purpose of housing the cooktop and providing an eating area. In that case, the fixture should be adjustable. It's also a good idea to install it with a dimmer, allowing you to control the level of light accordingly.

For this area, you'll need to position the light fixture in front of the cooktop to prevent glare.

Hanging fixtures can provide suitable task lighting over an island cooktop.

Accent and Decorative Lighting

Accent lighting draws attention to a particular element, such as an interesting architectural feature or decorative object. The key here is choosing what to highlight— a custom vent hood, an architectural feature, or the objects inside a glass-door cabinet. Use accent lighting to add personality to the room.

While accent lighting draws attention to an object or feature, decorative lighting draws attention to itself. It can be kinetic, in the form of candles or the glow from inside a fireplace, or static, such as a fixed wall candelabra. It doesn't highlight specific areas the way accent lighting does, and it doesn't provide a great deal of illumination as does ambient lighting, but decorative lighting is a device designers love to use.

Small spotlights inside glass-fronted cabinets, above, are one form of accent lighting. In the kitchen below, small spotlights, hidden by the cabinets' crown molding, are used to up-light the soffit area.

Accent lights can be used to highlight an architectural feature, such as the space above this kitchen's dropped ceiling.

In a kitchen with all-white cabinets and surfaces and lots of glass and metal, reflected light must be taken into account. **Far right:** Because this small kitchen receives very little natural light, generous lighting and an all-white scheme seemed logical. Small spotlights and several small pendants provide the room with adequate illumination. Keeping the wattage low avoids the pitfall of harsh glare.

    Top right: Compact under-cabinet lights reflect beauti-

it's in the
details *

fully on the marble backsplash and counter.
    Bottom right: Illuminated glass cabinets showcase the owners' fine china and glassware.

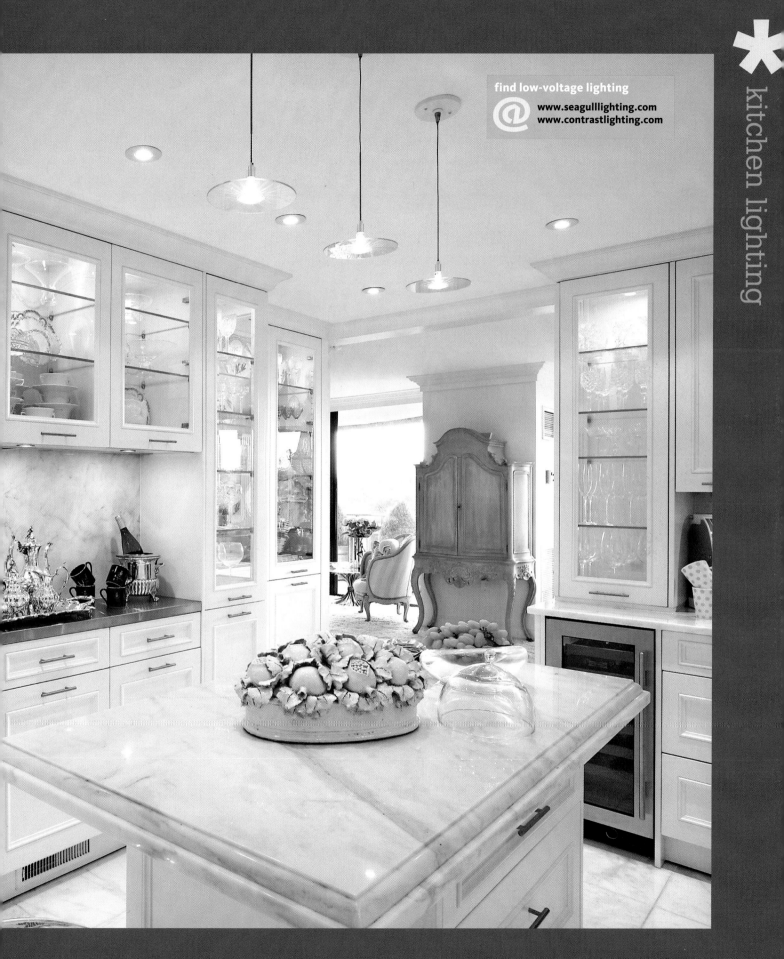

Lighting Fixtures

For general illumination, ceiling fixtures, such as recessed canister lights, are a good choice. Pendants, small spotlights, and fluorescent strips can all be used for task lighting. You can also create accent lighting with small spotlights, as well as with track lights and rail systems.

Fixtures play a role in the kitchen's decor, too, and come in a wide range of styles and finishes.

A pair of metal-shaded pendants, opposite, have a nostalgic look that's perfect for a cottage-style kitchen. Barrel shades on this three-arm fixture, left, have midcentury Modern appeal. A ceiling fixture over the table, above, adds to the contemporary style of the overall design.

Creating a specific style in a kitchen means getting all of the details right—down to the lighting fixtures. **Far right:** This French-country kitchen glows in the warmth of creamy color cabinets, mellow wood tones, and perfect lighting. Bronze-colored reproduction hanging lanterns supplement the ambient light; at night they can be dimmed low to set a quiet mood.

Top right: Wall-mounted lanterns draw attention to a cozy nook, and a

it's in the details *

pretty chandelier adds flair above the table.
Bottom right: Casement windows with grilles over a farmhouse sink bring in the morning light.

find French-country fixtures

@ www.ballarddesigns.com
www.lampsplus.com

I want to use recessed fixtures for overall lighting in my new kitchen, but I don't want the "Swiss cheese" effect on my ceiling. Help!

what the experts say

The American Lighting Association (ALA) says, "General lighting can be achieved with either recessed lighting or a central, decorative chandelier. Recessed lighting is best placed around the perimeter of the room and approximately 30 inches away from the wall. Chandeliers can be used in addition to other lighting in the space."

The idea is to create a consistent spread of light. If the light breaks into a noticeable pattern, the sources are placed too far apart.

what real people do

Today, most people use more than one fixture. According to the ALA, "Lighting over the kitchen table is multipurpose. A decorative pendant will provide sufficient task lighting while also adding a touch of style and personality to your space."

Mount pendant fixtures so that they hang 30 inches above the tabletop. If your table is round, the fixture should ideally be 12 inches narrower than the diameter of the table. For square and rectangular tables, choose a fixture that is 12 inches narrower than the smallest side.

Island counters and breakfast bars demand a combination of task and general lighting. Mount each pendant so that the bottom of the shade is approximately 66 inches above the floor.

Using more than one type of light gives this kitchen added interest and improves function.

STEP 1 examine your activities

Make a list of everything that occurs in your kitchen on a daily basis. Besides typical kitchen duties, such as cooking meals and cleaning up, include your hobby or craft pursuits and anything else you do—or would like to do—in the kitchen, such as clipping coupons, paying bills, reading the paper, or doing crafts. Be sure to consult other family members. Undoubtedly, there will be lots of things on your list, which only makes the lighting choices more critical. If your list gets too long, group similar tasks.

STEP 2 sketch a plan

Make a sketch of your kitchen's floor plan, and circle various zones or activity centers. Mark each circle with a G for general, or ambient, light, T for task light, A for accent light, and D for decorative light. In some places, you may want to indicate more than one. For example, if you plan on using your kitchen table for dining and for paying the bills, you might indicate A, G, and T. Identify your general lighting needs first, and then add your task lighting. Mark the spots for accent and decorative lighting on your plan last.

STEP 3 check local codes

Every municipality has strict regulations regarding the type of fixtures you can use and the placement of light and electricity around water. If you want to pass inspection, be sure you don't violate codes by specifying a lamp that isn't allowed in your area or by installing a fixture too close to an area that's exposed to water.

If you are going to use compact fluorescent bulbs (CFLs), find out how to dispose of used ones. These bulbs are energy efficient, but they also contain mercury. You may have to take them to a hazardous-waste center.

STEP 4 visit showrooms

The best way to learn about your options is to visit lighting showrooms. You can often take advantage of free in-store consultations. If your plan is complicated or if you have questions that require at-home consultation, you may be pleasantly surprised at the modest fee charged by a lighting specialist.

Be sure to take your sketch with your informal lighting plan along with you. However, if planning light for your kitchen seems too complicated, you can hire a lighting designer or consult your architect.

chapter 8

kitchen style

- ◆ **STYLE, PLEASE**
- ◆ **COLOR BASICS**
- ◆ **THOROUGHLY MODERN**
- ◆ **TRADITIONAL AND TIMELESS**
- ◆ **NOTABLY NOSTALGIC**
- ◆ **OLD WORLD VALUES**

Kitchens simply have to be stylish today. After all, they are the center of our home universe, and we do a lot of living in them. While you are planning your new kitchen, its zoned-to-perfection floor plan, great new cabinets, and sparkling new appliances, give some thought to how you want to pull all of these aspects together comfortably and aesthetically. Color is key, but so are the many details that signal your personal style.

Are you a traditionalist, a modernist, or something in between? Take a look and find out.

Style, Please

Not sure what style is best for you? Not to worry. The first thing to do is visit a kitchen showroom or a home-improvement center. There you'll find setups of different cabinets with countertops, backsplashes, and sinks in place to give you an idea of what goes together. This is a good way to see what's in style and what appeals to you. You can also talk to someone there who will be able to show you different finishes, materials, door styles, and so forth.

You would be wise to read design magazines and to cut out photographs of kitchens that you like. Bring these with you when you're shopping. And don't forget about TV; you can see some of the latest design trends and products on home-improvement shows. You can also visit the networks' Web sites.

Another excellent source of inspiration is to attend a decorator showhouse, which is typically a charity event and usually happens in the fall or spring. You'll not only get ideas from the house itself, but you may be able to meet some of the design professionals whose work is on display. The fee to attend is usually affordable—about $25—and worth it.

This pretty kitchen and dining area, above and opposite, may not be large, but it's big on style. A warm neutral color scheme is inviting, and furnishings are simple but elegant.

Color Basics

Color has amazing properties. It can evoke memories, create a mood, or even change your perception of space. Light colors expand a room, while darker colors draw the walls inward. If you have a high ceiling and feel that the room lacks coziness, paint the ceiling a shade deeper than the walls.

Most people prefer to keep fixtures and permanent features, such as cabinets and countertops, neutral, applying color to the walls and adding one or two color accents. But some fearless folk don't shy away from an unabashedly bold palette. And although it is strictly a matter of personal preference, most designers will tell you to use no more than three colors in one room. There really can be too much of a good thing.

For a lively look, use two or three colors, combining unequal amounts and different shades of each one. Include a neutral. If you don't, your eyes won't know where to focus. Let one color dominate. If you're more tentative, try a monochromatic (one color) scheme.

Remember, even professionals have color mishaps. Always do a color test on part of the wall, looking at it in daylight and at night, before painting the room.

A color—even white—isn't just a color; it has numerous tones and shades. The creamy off-white on the cabinets, opposite, is slightly yellow. A bold blue, below, dominates this kitchen design.

Thoroughly Modern

You may often see the words "modern" and "contemporary" used interchangeably. But to be precise, Modern is a style unto itself with roots in the early to mid-twentieth century. It's sparce—no Victorian frills—sleek, geometric, and somewhat high-tech. Contemporary actually refers to what is of the moment—the style of *now*.

If you like clean lines and a minimum of ornamentation, you are a Modernist. The architecture is spare and right-angled—no decorative trimwork or graceful arches. Materials tend to be industrial—metal and glass—but contemporary interpreters of the style have added warmth, using some color and wood to make the look less severe. Cabinets without a face frame and with flat-panel doors and drawers fill the bill in medium to deep finishes.

Plain casement windows, left, and synthetic materials, such as the quartz-composite countertops, top, are compatible with Modern design. The frameless cabinets, often called "European style," have concealed hinges, above, for a streamlined appearance.

Traditional style is formal. The breakfast area, above, is a bit more casual than the kitchen proper, opposite, but the details, such as the trimwork and flooring, unify the overall look.

Traditional and Timeless

Traditional style has elements of English and American eighteenth- and early-nineteenth-century design. The look is rich and formal with architectural elements such as graceful arches, columns, trimwork, and double-hung windows with muntins or any divided-light window.

To create the look, select wood cabinetry, finished in a mellow wood stain or painted white, with fine furniture details. The cabinets' door style should be a raised-panel design. Hardware that evokes the mood of the period will add the right touch.

An updated version of this look is called "transitional style." It isn't quite as formal, nor does it lean too much toward a contemporary look. If you're a middle-of-the-road type when it comes to decorating, blending elements of the past with those of today is your style.

Notably Nostalgic

Call it "cottage" or "Victorian," this look recalls the turn of the last century, with a bit of a modern twist. It's certainly much less formal and a lot less cluttered than its inspiration, but it still strikes a nostalgic note, particularly in terms of fixtures, cabinets, and hardware. Cabinets are painted, and usually white. The door style is flat panel—a plainer version of the type of door you'd expect in a traditional-style room—and drawer and door hardware may be a simple reproduction knob in glass, porcelain, or metal.

Wall treatments could include painted paneling, in particular bead-board, wainscoting and a chair rail, or subway-style tiles.

A few contemporary touches keep a nostalgic look from becoming too cutesy. You could do this with a contemporary light fixture or window treatment.

A mixture of old and new is today's version of cottage, country, or Victorian style. Less formal than traditional, this kitchen, above and opposite, evokes the past with simple cabinetry and furnishings. But the high-tech appliances and modern pendants keep it firmly grounded in the present.

A spectacular cooking center at one end of this kitchen has the look and warmth of an enormous hearth. The tiled backsplash, the hood, the carved molding, and the candle sconces are important style details.

Old World Values

Elements of the Old World inspired this decorative style, which may be highly formal with references to classical Greece and Rome or to the timeless, earthy dwellings of the European countryside, notably France, Italy, and Spain.

Unlike Modern architecture with its rectilinear windows and doorways, true Old World design features arches and curves, and windows with either divided lights or grilles.

Wood cabinetry, often freestanding or with an unfitted appearance, is heavy with carving and ornate molding. Rustic finishes on metal hardware and faucets are highly appropriate. Stone and tile surfaces are at home here, and backsplashes may convey an Old World motif in mosaic or handpainted tile. A decorative range hood adds the appeal of a country hearth.

Take your color cues from the tones in the wood, the stone, and the warm sunny climates that have inspired Old World style. And include a few decorative accents with hand-painted tile, folk art, or pottery.

The ceiling's wood beams with carved corbels play an immense role in establishing the room's architectural style. Cabinetry with an unfitted appearance enhances the sense of Old World living.

STEP 1 make a sample board

Try out your ideas on a sample board first. To make one, use a 2 x 4-foot sheet of ½-inch plywood, which is heavy enough to hold your samples but light enough for you to handle. Mount the samples on the board. Include paint and wood-stain chips, fabric swatches, and flooring, tile, and countertop samples. The board lets you test ideas before you start buying materials and make costly mistakes. Try different combinations of colors and patterns. Look at them under all types of light, night and day. Add photographs of cabinets, fixtures, and appliances. Record manufacturer and retail sources, too.

STEP 2 note your sight lines

A sight line is the visual path the eye follows from a given point within a room or from an entrance. A room's primary sight line is at the entry. It is the most important one because it draws your attention into the room. Your eye immediately moves in one direction toward whatever is directly opposite the doorway. Very often in a kitchen it is the sink or the range. If your sight lines are not as you wish them to be, the time for relocating fixtures and appliances is not at the decorating stage. However, if you're still in the planning process, rethink your floor plan to see what you may be able to move.

resource guide

The following list of manufacturers and associations is meant to be a general guide to additional industry and product-related sources. It is not intended as a listing of products and manufacturers represented by the photographs in this book.

MANUFACTURERS

Above View
414-744-7118
www.aboveview.com
Makes ornamental plaster ceiling tiles.

Adagio, Inc.
877-988-2297
www.adagiosinks.com
Makes hand-crafted sinks in a variety of materials.

Almillmo
201-820-4540
www.allmilmo-us.com
Manufactures kitchen furniture.

Amana
800-616-2664
www.amana.com
Manufactures refrigerators, dishwashers, and cooking appliances.

American Standard
800-442-1902
www.americanstandard-us.com
Manufactures plumbing and tile products.

Amerock
800-435-6959
www.amerock.com
Manufactures cabinet hardware.

Andersen
800-426-4261
www.andersenwindows.com
Manufactures an extensive range of window and skylight styles; also carries a selection of patio doors.

Ann Sacks Tile and Stone, part of the Kohler Company
800-278-8453
www.annsacks.com
Manufactures a broad line of tile and stone, including terra-cotta and mosaics.

Armstrong World Industries
717-397-0611
www.armstrong.com
Manufactures floors, cabinets, and ceilings for both residential and commercial use.

Artemide
631-694-9292
www.artemide.com
Manufactures lighting fixtures.

Artistic Tile
877-528-5401
www.artistictile.com
Manufactures various types of tile, including stone, porcelain, and ceramic.

Ballard Designs
800-536-7551
www.ballarddesigns.com
Manufactures furniture, wall decor, lighting, and rugs.

Bar Stools & Barstools
800-926-4006
www.bar-stools-barstools.com
Distributes bar stools, furniture, and chairs.

Benjamin Moore & Co.
www.benjaminmoore.com
Manufactures paint.

Big Chill Refrigerators
877-842-3269
www.bigchillfridge.com
Manufactures retro-style refrigerators.

Blanco America
www.blancoamerica.com
Manufactures sinks and faucets.

BSH Home Appliances Corporation
714-901-6600
www.boschappliances.com
Manufactures major and small appliances.

Brewster Home Fashions
781-963-4800
www.brewsterwallcovering.com
Manufactures wallpaper, fabrics, and borders
in many patterns and styles.

Bruce Hardwood Floors,
Div. of Armstrong World Industries
800-233-3823
www.bruce.com
Manufactures hardwood flooring.

Buying Bar Stools
877-379-6966
www.buying-bar-stools.com
Distributes bar stools, home bars, and liquor
cabinets.

CaesarStone USA
818-779-0999
www.caesarstoneus.com
Manufactures quartz-composite countertops.

Country Curtains
800-937-1237
www.countrycurtains.com
A national retailer and online source for ready-made
curtains, draperies, shades, blinds, hardware, and
accessories.

Corian, a div. of DuPont
800-441-7515
www.corian.com
Manufactures solid-surfacing material for residential
and commercial kitchens.

Crossville, Inc.
931-484-2110
www.crossvilleinc.com
Manufactures porcelain, stone, and metal tile.

Dacor
800-793-0093
www.dacor.com
Manufactures wall ovens, cooktops, ranges, and
other kitchen appliances.

Delta Faucet Co.
800-345-3358
www.deltafaucet.com
Manufactures a variety of faucets and finishes for
kitchens and baths.

Dex Industries
404-753-0600
www.dexstudios.com
Creates custom concrete sinks and countertops.

Elkay
630-574-8484
www.elkayusa.com
Manufactures sinks, faucets, and countertops.

Enviro-Trash Concepts
A subsidiary of the Starco Company, LLC
866-671-8878
www.envirotrashconcepts.com
Manufactures an eco-friendly line of trash systems.

Fisher and Paykel
888-936-7872
www.fisherpaykel.com
Manufactures kitchen appliances.

Florida Tile
800-352-8453
www.floridatile.com
Distributor and manufacturer of ceramic wall
and floor tile.

Formica Corporation
800-367-6422
www.formica.com
Manufactures plastic laminate and solid-surfacing
material.

Frigidaire
800-374-4432
www.frigidaire.com
Manufacturers major appliances, including ranges,
cooktops, refrigerators, and dishwashers.

Franke
www.franke.com
Manufactures faucets and plumbed systems including
beverage and coffee stations.

General Electric
800-626-2005
www.geappliances.com
Manufactures refrigerators, dishwashers, ovens,
and other major appliances.

Glidden
800-454-3336
www.glidden.com
Manufactures paint.

Green Mountain Soapstone Corp.
800-585-5636
www.greenmountainsoapstone.com
Manufactures soapstone floors, walls, sinks,
and countertops.

Google SketchUp
http://sketchup.google.com
Downloadable 3-D modeling software.

Haier America
877-337-3639
www.haieramerica.com
Manufactures electronics and appliances,
including wine cellars.

Hammered Hinges
610-745-0009
www.hammeredhinges.com
Handmade wrought-iron cabinet hardware, hinges,
pulls, and latches.

IKEA
217-347-7701
www.ikea.com
Sells their home furnishings, kitchen appliances,
cabinets, sinks, faucets, and countertops nationwide.

Italian Trade Commission
Ceramic Tile Dept.
212-980-1500
www.italytile.com
An organization that promotes Italian tile, offering
consumers a guide to buying Italian ceramic tile.

Jenn-Air
A division of Maytag
800-536-6247
www.jennair.com
Manufactures major kitchen appliances including
cooktops, ranges, and ovens.

John Boos
217-347-7701
www.johnboos.com
Manufactures butcher block cutting boards and
countertops, and stainless-steel products.

Kemiko Concrete Products
903-587-3708
www.kemiko.com
Manufactures acid stains for concrete flooring
and other concrete products; creates decorative
concrete floors.

Kitchenaid
800-541-6390
www.kitchenaid.com
Manufactures kitchen appliances and accessories.

Kohler
800-456-4537
www.kohlerco.com
Manufactures kitchen and bath sinks, faucets, and related accessories.

Kliptech
253-507-4622
www.kliptech.com
Manufactures eco-friendly countertops made from recycled paper, recycled wood fiber, and plantation-grown bamboo fiber.

KraftMaid Cabinetry
888-562-7744
www.kraftmaid.com
Manufactures stock and built-to-order cabinets with a variety of finishes and storage options.

Lamps Plus
800-782-1967
www.lampsplus.com
Online source for lighting fixtures.

LG
800-243-0000
www.lge.com
Manufactures major appliances.

Lightology
773-883-6111
www.lightology.com
Manufactures lighting fixtures.

Maytag Corp.
800-344-1274
www.maytag.com
Manufactures major appliances.

Miele
800-843-7231
www.miele.com
Manufactures major appliances.

Moen
440-962-2000
www.moen.com
Manufactures faucets, sinks, and accessories for both kitchens and baths.

Mosaic Source
562-598-3143
www.mosaicsource.com
Online source for mosaic and recycled-glass tiles.

Murray Feiss
800-969-3347
www.feiss.com
Manufactures ceiling lights, chandeliers, and lamps.

My Granite Care
952-200-2727
www.mygranitecare.com
Provides information on maintaining granite surfaces.

Native Trails
800-786-0862
www.nativetrails.net
A source for handcrafted copper sinks and Talavera tiles.

Pfister Faucets
800-732-8238
www.pfisterfaucets.com
Manufactures faucets.

Plain & Fancy Custom Cabinetry
800-447-9006
www.plainfancycabinetry.com
Makes custom cabinetry.

Pyrolave USA
919-788-8953
www.pyrolave.com
Manufactures glazed lava-stone countertops.

Rejuvenation

888-401-1900

www.rejuvenation.com

Manufactures kitchen hardware and light fixtures.

Rocky Mountain Hardware

888-788-2013

www.rockymountainhardware.com

Online source for hardware accessories for the home including kitchen, bath, and window hardware.

Seagull Lighting Products, Inc.

800-877-4855

www.seagulllighting.com

Manufactures lighting fixtures.

Sharp USA

800-237-4277

www.sharpusa.com

Manufactures electronics and small appliances.

Sherwin-Williams

www.sherwin-williams.com

Manufactures paint.

SieMatic-USA

215-604-1350

www.siematic.com

Manufactures "fitted" kitchens and kitchen furniture.

Sonoma Cast Stone

877-939-9929

www.sonomastone.com

Designs and casts concrete sinks and countertops.

Sub-Zero

800-222-7820

www.subzero.com

Manufactures refrigerators and freezers in full sizes and as modular units.

Thermador

800-735-4328

www.thermador.com

Manufactures appliances for cooking, refrigeration, and dishwashing.

Thibaut Inc.

800-223-0704

www.thibautdesign.com

Manufactures wallpaper and fabrics.

Viking Range Corp.

888-845-4641

www.vikingrange.com

Manufactures professional-style kitchen appliances.

Watermark Designs, Ltd.

800-842-7277

www.watermark-designs.com

Manufactures faucets and lighting fixtures.

Wilsonart International, Inc.

800-433-3222

www.wilsonart.com

Manufactures solid-surfacing material; plastic laminate; and adhesive for kitchen countertops, cabinets, floors, and fixtures.

Wolf Appliance Company

800-222-7820

www.wolfappliance.com

Manufactures professional-style cooking appliances.

Wood-Mode Fine Custom Cabinetry

877-635-7500

www.wood-mode.com

Manufactures custom cabinetry for the kitchen.

Woodworkers Hardware

800-383-0130

www.wwhardware.com

Supplies cabinet hardware.

York Wallcoverings

717-846-4456

www.yorkwall.com

Manufactures wallpaper and borders.

Zodiaq

a div. of DuPont

800-441-7515

www.zodiaq.com

Manufactures quartz-composite countertops.

ASSOCIATIONS

American Society of Interior Designers (ASID)

202-546-3480

www.asid.org

A professional organization of interior designers offering referral services to consumers.

Freecycle

www.freecycle.org

A nonprofit movement to reuse items within communities for free.

Green Building Certification Institute (GBCI)

440-250-9222

www.gbci.org

A professional organization dedicated to green building practices.

International Furnishings and Design Association (IFDA)

610-535-6422

www.ifda.com

A professional organization representing furnishings and design professionals.

International Interior Design Association (IIDA)

888-799-4432

www.iida.com

A professional organization for interior design professionals.

National Association of Remodeling Industry (NARI)

800-611-6274

www.nari.org

A professional organization for remodelers, contractors, and design/remodelers; also offers consumer information.

National Kitchen and Bath Association (NKBA)

800-843-6522

www.nkba.org

A national trade organization for kitchen and bath design professionals; offers consumers product information and a referral service.

National Public Health and Safety Company (NSF)

1-800-673-8010

www.nsf.org

Certifies products and writes standards for food, water, and consumer goods.

Tile Council Of America

864-646-8453

www.tileusa.com

A trade organization dedicated to promoting the tile industry; also provides consumer information for selecting and installing tile.

DESIGNERS

Helene Goodman, IIDA
Interior Design

723-747-8502

hgoodman@comcast.net

Susan Obercian
European Country Kitchens

973-218-9004

www.eckitchens.com

Lucianna Samu

www.reallyathome.com

lu@luciannasamu.com

glossary

Absorption (light): The light energy (wavelengths) not reflected by an object or substance. The color of a substance depends on the wavelength reflected.

Accent lighting: A type of light that highlights an area or object to emphasize that aspect of a room's character.

Accessible design: Design that accommodates persons with physical disabilities.

Adaptable design: Design that can be easily changed to accommodate a person with disabilities.

Ambient light: General illumination that surrounds a room. There is no visible source of the light.

Appliance garage: Countertop storage for small appliances.

Apron: The front panel of a sink that may or may not be exposed.

Awning window: A window with a single framed-glass panel. It is hinged at the top to swing out when it is open.

Backlighting: Illumination coming from a source behind or at the side of an object.

Backsplash: The finish material that covers the wall behind a countertop. The backsplash can be attached to the countertop or separate from it.

Baking center: An area near an oven(s) and a refrigerator that contains a countertop for rolling out dough and storage for baking supplies.

Barrier-free fixture: A fixture specifically designed to allow access to people who use wheelchairs or who have limited mobility.

Base cabinet: A cabinet that rests on the floor under a countertop.

Base plan: A map of an existing room that shows detailed measurements and locations of fixtures, appliances, and other permanent elements.

Basin: A shallow sink.

Built-in: A cabinet, shelf, medicine chest, or other storage unit that is recessed into the wall.

Bump out: Living space created by cantilevering the floor and ceiling joists (or adding to a floor slab) and extending the exterior wall of a room.

Butcher block: A counter or table-top material composed of strips of hardwood, often rock maple, laminated together and sealed against moisture.

Candlepower (Cp): The intensity of light measured at a lamp. This term is generally used for task and accent lighting.

Cantilever: A structural beam supported on one end. A cantilever can be used to support a small addition.

Casement window: A window that consists of one framed-glass panel that is hinged on the side. It swings outward from the opening at the turn of a crank.

Centerline: The dissecting line through the center of an object, such as a sink.

CFM: An abbreviation that refers to the amount of cubic feet of air that is moved per minute by an exhaust fan.

Chair rail: A decorative wall molding installed midway between the floor and ceiling. Traditionally, chair rails protected walls from damage from chair backs.

Cleanup center: The area of a kitchen where the sink, waste-disposal unit, trash compactor, dishwasher, and related accessories are grouped for easy access and efficient use.

Clearance: The space between two fixtures, the centerlines of two fixtures, or a fixture and an obstacle, such as a wall. Clearances may be mandated by codes.

Code: A locally or nationally enforced mandate regarding structural design, materials, plumbing, or electrical systems that states what you can or cannot do when you build or remodel. Codes are intended to protect standards of health, safety, and land use.

Color intensity: Strength or saturation of a color.

Color rendition index (CRI): Measures the way a light source renders color. The higher the number, the more the color resembles how it appears in sunlight.

Combing: A painting technique that involves using a small device with teeth or grooves over a wet painted surface to create a grained effect.

Contemporary style: A style of decoration or architecture that is modern and pertains to what is current.

Cooking center: The kitchen area where the cooktop, oven(s), and food preperation surfaces, appliances, and utensils are grouped.

Correlated color temperature (CCT): Compares the apparent warmth or coolness of discontinuous-spectrum light.

Countertop: The work surface of a counter, island, or peninsula, usually 36 inches high. Common countertop materials include granite, slate, marble, plastic laminate, and solid-surfacing material.

Cove lights: Lights that reflect upward, sometimes located on top of wall cabinets.

Crown molding: A decorative molding usually installed where the wall and ceiling meet.

Dimmer Switch: A switch that can vary the intensity of the light source that it controls.

Double-hung window: A window that consists of two framed-glass panels that slide open vertically, guided by a metal or wood track.

Downlighting: A lighting technique that illuminates objects or areas from above.

Duct: A tube or passage for venting indoor air to the outside.

Faux painting: Various painting techniques that mimic wood, marble, and other stone.

Fittings: The plumbing devices that transport water to the fixtures. These can include faucets, sprayers, and spouts. Also pertains to hardware and some accessories, such as soap dispensers and instant-water dispensers.

Fixed window: A window that cannot be opened. It is usually a decorative unit, such as a half-round or Palladian-style window.

Fixture: Any fixed part of the structural design, such as sinks.

Fixture spacing: Refers to how far apart to space ambient-light fixtures for an even field of light.

Fluorescent lamp: An energy-efficient light source made of a tube with an interior phosphorus coating that glows when energized by electricity.

Foot-candle (Fc): A unit used to measure the brightness produced by a lamp. A foot-candle is equal to one lumen per square foot of surface.

Framed cabinets: Cabinets with a full frame across the face of the cabinet box.

Frameless cabinets: European-style cabinets without a face frame.

Glazing (walls): A technique for applying a thinned, tinted wash of translucent color to a dry undercoat of paint.

Ground-fault circuit interrupter (GFCI): A safety circuit breaker that compares the amount of current entering a receptacle with the amount leaving. If there is a discrepancy of 0.005 volt, the GFCI breaks the circuit in a fraction of a second. GFCIs are required by the National Electrical Code in areas that are subject to dampness.

Grout: A binder and filler applied in the joints between ceramic tile.

Halogen bulb: A bulb filled with halogen gas, a substance that causes the particles of tungsten to be redeposited onto the tungsten filament. This process extends the lamp's life and makes the light whiter and brighter.

Hardware: Wood, metal, or plastic trim found on the exterior of furniture or cabinetry, such as knobs, handles, and decorative trim.

Highlight: The lightest tone in a room.

Incandescent lamp: A bulb that contains a conductive filament through which current flows. The current reacts with an inert gas inside the bulb, which makes the filament glow.

Intensity: Strength of a color.

Island: A base cabinet and countertop unit that stands independent from walls so that there is access from all four sides.

Kitchen fans: Fans that remove grease, moisture, smoke, and heat from the kitchen.

Lazy Susan: Axis-mounted shelves that revolve. Also called carousel shelves.

Load-bearing wall: A wall that supports a structure's vertical load. Openings in any load-bearing wall must be reinforced to carry the live and dead weight of the structure's load.

Low-voltage lights: Lights that operate on 12 to 50 volts rather than the standard 120 volts used in most homes.

Lumen: A term that refers to the intensity of light measured at a light source that is used for general or ambient lighting.

Muntins: Framing members of a window that divide the panes of glass.

Nonbearing wall: An interior wall that provides no structural support for any portion of the house.

Palette: A range of colors that complement one another.

Peninsula: A countertop, with or without a base cabinet, which is connected at one end to a wall or another countertop and extends outward, providing access on three sides.

Proportion: The relationship of one object to another.

Recessed light fixtures: Light fixtures that are installed into ceilings, soffits, or cabinets and are flush with the surrounding area.

Refacing: Replacing the doors and drawers on cabinets and covering the frame with a matching material.

Reflectance levels: The amount of light that is reflected from a colored surface, such as a tile wall or painted surface.

Roof window: A horizontal window that is installed on the roof. Roof windows are ventilating.

Scale: The size of a room or object.

Schematic: A detailed diagram of systems (such as plumbing or electrical) within a home.

Sconce: A decorative wall bracket, sometimes made of iron or glass, that shields a bulb.

Secondary work center: An area of the kitchen where extra activity is done, such as laundry or baking.

Semicustom cabinets: Cabinets that are available in specific sizes but with a wide variety of options.

Sight line: The natural line of sight the eye travels when looking into or around a room.

Skylight: A framed opening in the roof that admits sunlight into the house. It can be covered with either a flat glass panel or a plastic dome.

Sliding window: Similar to a double-hung window turned on its side. The glass panels slide horizontally.

Snap-in grilles: Ready-made rectangular and diamond-pattern grilles that snap into a window sash and create the look of a true divided-light window.

Solid-surfacing countertop: A countertop material made of acrylic plastic and fine-ground synthetic particles, sometimes made to look like natural stone.

Soffit: The area just below the ceiling and above the wall cabinets. It may be boxed in or open.

Space reconfiguration: A design term that is used to describe the reallocation of interior space without adding on.

Spout: The tube or pipe from which water gushes out of a faucet.

Stock cabinets: Cabinets that are in stock or available quickly when ordered from a retail outlet.

Subfloor: The flooring applied directly to the floor joists on top of which the finished floor rests.

Task lighting: Lighting designed to illuminate a particular task, such as chopping.

Tone: The degree of lightness or darkness of a color.

Trompe l'oeil: French for "fool the eye." A paint technique that creates a photographically real illusion of space or objects.

True divided-light window: A window composed of multiple glass panes that are divided by and held together by muntins.

Under-cabinet light fixtures: Task lights that are installed on the undersides of cabinets.

Universal design: Products and designs that are easy to use by people of all ages, heights, and varying physical abilities.

Wainscoting: Paneling that extends 36 to 42 inches or so upward from the floor level, over the finished wall surface. It is often finished with a horizontal strip of molding mounted at the proper height and protruding enough to prevent the top of a chair back from touching a wall surface.

Wall cabinet: A cabinet, usually 12 inches deep, that's mounted on the wall a minimum of 15 inches above a countertop.

Work triangle: The area bounded by the lines that connect the sink, range, and refrigerator.

Xenon bulb: A bulb similar to a halogen bulb, except that it is filled with xenon gas and does not emit ultraviolet (UV) rays. In addition, it is cooler and more energy efficient.

index

photo credits

page 1: Bob Greenspan, stylist: Susan Andrews **page 2:** Mark Lohman **page 5:** Mark Lohman, design: Roxanne Packham Design **page 7:** Eric Roth **page 9:** Mark Lohman **pages 10–13:** davidduncanlivingston.com **pages 14–15:** *both* Julian Wass, design: Jonathan Adler Interior Design **page 16:** *both* Julian Wass, design: Angie Hranowski Design Studio **page 17:** *both* Julian Wass, design: Hein + Cozzi Inc. **pages 18–19:** *all* Peter Rymwid Photography, design: Helene Goodman IIDA **pages 20–21:** *all* Olson Photographic, LLC, design: Jack Rosen Custom Kitchens **pages 22–23:** *both* Mark Lohman **pages 24–25:** *all* Mark Lohman, top left architect: Michael Lee Architects, bottom left design: Michelle McCauley, right design: Roxanne Packham Design **page 26:** courtesy of IKEA **pages 28–29:** *all* Olson Photographic, LLC **pages 30–31:** Mark Samu, architect: Ellen Roche AIA **pages 32–33:** *all* davidduncanlivingston.com **pages 34–35:** *all* Stacy Bass **pages 36–37:** *all* Bob Greenspan, stylist: Susan Andrews **pages 38–39:** *all* Tony Giammarino/Giammarino & Dworkin, design: BowmansWoodworking.com **page 41:** *both* Mark Lohman, design: Haefele Design **pages 42–43:** *all* davidduncanlivingston.com **pages 44–45:** *both* Mark Lohman **pages 46–47:** *both* Joseph De Leo **pages 48–49:** Olson Photographic, LLC, design: Cole Harris Associates **pages 50–51:** *all* Mark Lohman, design: Taddey Karlin Design **pages 53–55:** *all* davidduncanlivingston.com **pages 57–59:** *all* Tony Giammarino/Giammarino & Dworkin **page 60:** Bob Greenspan, stylist: Susan Andrews **page 62:** Paul Castello **page 63:** Mark Samu design: Beach Glass Design **pages 64–65:** Eric Roth, design: bkarch.com **page 66:** courtesy of Merillat **page 67:** *top* courtesy of Merillat; *bottom* Eric Roth, design: sternmccafferty.com **pages 68–69:**

all davidduncanlivingston.com **pages 70–71:** *all* Eric Roth, design: Water & Fire Kitchen Design **pages 72–73:** *all* courtesy of Merillat **pages 74–75:** *left* Mark Samu, design: Suzette O'Farrell Design; *bottom right* Mark Samu; *top right* Mark Lohman, design: Ursula Beatt **pages 76–79:** Tony Giammarino/Giammarino & Dworkin, design: homemasons.com **page 80:** davidduncanlivingston.com **page 81:** *top* davidduncanlivingston.com; Mark Lohman, architect: Nicholas Budd Architects **pages 82–83:** *all* Eric Roth, design: nicholaeff.com **page 85:** Olson Photographic, LLC, design Cucina Designs, Branford, CT **page 86:** *top* courtesy of Caesarstone; *bottom* Mark Samu, design: Really at Home **page 87:** *left* Eric Roth, design Anamika Design; *right* Bob Greenspan, stylist: Susan Andrews **page 88:** *left* davidduncanlivingston.com **pages 88–89:** Anne Gummerson, design: Designline **page 89:** *right* Tony Giammarino/Giammarino & Dworkin, design: Kate Cooper **page 90:** *top* courtesy of CaesarStone Quartz Surfaces; *bottom* courtesy of Caesarstone, architect: Dennis Gibbens Architects **page 91:** courtesy of Caesarstone, architect: Dennis Gibbens Architects **page 92:** davidduncanlivingston.com **page 93:** *top* Eric Roth, design GFCDevelopment; *bottom* davidduncanlivingston.com **page 94:** *both* courtesy of Teragren Fine Bamboo Flooring, Countertops & Panels **Page 95:** melabee m miller, design Diane Romanowski **page 96–97:** *all* courtesy of Icestone **page 98–99:** *all* Mark Samu, design Ellen Roche AIA **page 100:** Tony Giammarino/Giammarino & Dworkin, design: homemasons.com **page 101:** Mark Lohman, design Haefele Design **page 102:** Bob Greenspan, stylist: Susan Andrews **page 103:** *top* Mark Samu, Blairhouse Interiors; *bottom* Mark Samu **pages 104–105:** *all* Bob Greenspan, stylist: Susan Andrews

page 106: *left* Tony Giammarino/Giammarino & Dworkin, design: Chris Siderio; *right* davidduncanlivingston.com **page 107:** davidduncanlivingston.com **page 108:** *top* courtesy of Teragren Fine Bamboo Flooring, Countertops & Panels; *bottom* Eric Roth **page 109:** *both* Mark Lohman **pages 110–111:** *all* courtesy of Armstrong **page 112:** *top* Eric Roth; *bottom* Eric Roth, design: www.jwconstructioninc.com **page 113:** *left* Eric Roth; *right* Bob Greenspan **page 115:** Stacy Bass **page 116:** *left* melabee m miller, design: Diane Romanowski; *right* Bob Greenspan, stylist: Susan Andrews **Page 117:** *top* Bob Greenspan, stylist: Susan Andrews; *bottom* davidduncanlivingston.com **page 118:** *both* courtesy of Kohler **page 119:** *top* Tony Giammarino/Giammarino & Dworkin, design: Mona Chutz; *bottom* courtesy of Kohler **page 120:** *top* davidduncanlivingston.com; *middle* courtesy of Corian; *bottom* Mark Lohman **page 121:** courtesy of Kohler **page 122:** *left* Tony Giammarino/Giammarino & Dworkin, design: Juliet Prakken; *right* Mark Lohman, design Douglas Burdge Architects **page 123:** *left* Mark Samu; *right* Olson Photographic, LLC, design J Interiors, RI **page 124:** Mark Lohman **page 125:** *top* Olson Photographic, LLC, *bottom* Mark Samu **page 126:** Bob Greenspan, stylist: Susan Andrews **page 127:** *top* Mark Lohman, design: Haefele Design; *bottom* Stacy Bass **Page 128–129:** *all* Tony Giammarino/Giammarino & Dworkin, design: GwaltneyFleming.com **Page 130:** *left* Mark Lohman; *right* Olson Photographic, LLC, design: Hobbs, New Canaan, CT **page 131:** Anne Gummerson, design: Designline **pages 132–133:** *all* davidduncanlivingston.com **page 135:** Bob Greenspan, stylist: Susan Andrews **page 136:** *left* courtesy of Wolf; *right* Mark Samu **page 137:** Tony Giammarino/Giammarino & Dworkin pages 138–139: *all* courtesy of Wolf **page 140:** Beth Singer, design/build: Lafata Cabinets **page 141:** *top* Bob Greenspan, stylist: Susan Andrews; *bottom* Olson Photographic, LLC, design: RMS Construction, Stamford, CT **pages 142–143:** *all* Mark Lohman, design Cynthia Marks Interior Design **page 144:** *top* courtesy of Sub-Zero; *bottom* Mark Lohman **page 145:** Mark Lohman **page 146:** *both* Olson Photographic, LLC, design: Capitol designs, Germantown, MD **page 147:** courtesy of GE **page 148:** *left* Olson Photographic, LLC, design: Elizabeth Whitney Design Studio, Avon, CT; *top right* courtesy of Sub-Zero; *bottom right* courtesy of Maytag **page 149:** *left* Olson Photographic, LLC, design: Wormser & Associates, Westport, CT; *right* Anne Gummerson, architect: Hammond Wilson Architects **page 150:** *top left* Tony Giammarino/Giammarino & Dworkin; *bottom right* Eric Roth, design: www.brittadesign.com **page 151:** Eric Roth, design: geraldpomeroydesigngroup.com **pages 152–153:** Eric Roth, design: www.brittadesign.com **page 154:** *top right and bottom left* courtesy of Sub-Zero; *bottom right* Olson Photographic, LLC **page 155:** Olson Photographic, LLC, design: Jack Rosen Custom Kitchens, Rockville, MD **pages 156–157:** *all* courtesy of Maytag **page 159:** davidduncanlivingston.com **page 160:** Anne Gummerson, architect: Scarlett Breeding **page 161:** Mark Lohman **pages 162–163:** Anne Gummerson, builder: Taylor-Reed Builders **pages 164–165:** Mark Samu, design Beach Glass Design **pages 166–167:** Olson Photographic, LLC **pages 168–169:** davidduncanlivingston.com **page 170:** *both* Olson Photographic, LLC, design Putnam Kitchens, Greenwich, CT **page 171:** Olson Photographic, LLC, design Ricci Construction, Cheshire, CT **pages 172–173:** Olson Photographic, LLC, design Martin Custom Construction, Kensington, CT **page 174:** *top right* Beth Singer, design/build: Kitchen Studio; *bottom* Anne Gummerson, design/architect: Alt Breeding Schwarz Architects **page 175:** Anne Gummerson, design: Parameter **pages 176–177:** *all* Olson Photographic, LLC, design: Jack Rosen Custom Kitchens, Rockville, MD **page 178:** Eric Roth, design: John DeBastiani **page 179:** *both* Eric Roth **pages 180–181:** *all* Anne Gummerson, design: Donna Godwin, Godwin Design and Interiors **pages 182–183:** Anne Gummerson, design: Currentworks **page 184:** *left* Eric Roth, design: wellsfox.com; *right* Eric Roth **page 185:** *left* Eric Roth; *right* Eric Roth, design: www.carpentermacneille.com **page 187:** Anne Gummerson, architect: Melville Thomas Architects **pages 188–193:** *all* davidduncanlivingston.com **pages 194–195:** *both* Olson Photographic, LLC, design: Dalia Canora Design, Darien, CT **pages 196–197:** *both* davidduncanlivingston.com **pages 198–199:** *both* Mark Lohman, design Douglas Burdge Architects **page 200:** *both* davidduncanlivingston.com **page 201:** Mark Lohman **page 203:** courtesy of Kohler **page 206:** davidduncanlivingston.com **page 213:** Bob Greenspan, stylist: Susan Andrews **page 214:** Olson Photographic, LLC, design: Elizabeth Whitney Design Studio, Avon, CT **page 215:** davidduncanlivingston.com **page 219:** Mark Lohman **page 220:** Mark Lohman, design: Douglas Burdge Architects **page 223:** Mark Lohman

Have a gardening, decorating, or home improvement project?
Look for these and other fine Creative Homeowner books
wherever books are sold

BEST SIGNATURE KITCHENS

A showcase of kitchens from top designers around the country.

Over 250 photographs.
240 pp.
8¼" × 10⅞"
$19.95 (US)
$23.95 (CAN)
BOOK #: CH279510

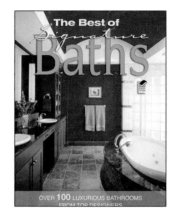

THE BEST OF SIGNATURE BATHS

Features luxurious and inspiring bathrooms from top designers.

Over 250 photographs.
240 pp.
8¼" × 10⅞"
$19.95 (US)
$21.95 (CAN)
BOOK #: CH279522

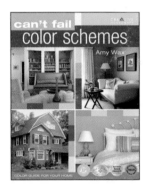

CAN'T FAIL COLOR SCHEMES

A take-it-with you visual guide to selecting color schemes and texture.

Over 300 photographs.
304 pp.
7" × 9¼"
$19.95 (US)
$21.95 (CAN)
BOOK #: CH279659

CAN'T FAIL COLOR SCHEMES—KITCHENS & BATHS

A guide to color ideas for kitchens and baths.

Over 300 photographs.
304 pp.
7" × 9¼"
$19.95 (US)
$21.95 (CAN)
BOOK #: CH279648

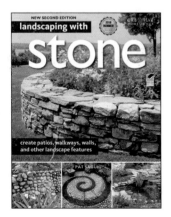

LANDSCAPING WITH STONE

Ideas for incorporating stone into the landscape.

Over 335 photographs.
224 pp.
8½" × 10⅞"
$19.95 (US)
$21.95 (CAN)
BOOK #: CH274179

SUCCESSFUL CONTAINER GARDENING

Information to grow your own flower, fruit, and vegetable "gardens."

Over 240 photographs.
160 pp.
8½" × 10⅞"
$14.95 (US)
$17.95 (CAN)
BOOK #: CH274857

For more information and to order direct, go to **www.creativehomeowner.com**